MONEY HACKS

MONEY HACKS

BECAUSE EVERYTHING YOU THINK YOU KNOW ABOUT MONEY IS WORING!

LARRY STEINHOUSE

An imprint of
Srishti Publishers & Distributors

Srishti Publishers & Distributors
A unit of AJR Publishing LLP
212A, Peacock Lane
Shahpur Jat, New Delhi – 110 049
editorial@srishtipublishers.com

First Published in India by Bold,
an imprint of Srishti Publishers & Distributors in 2023

First published by Morgan James Publishing in 2022

10 9 8 7 6 5 4 3 2

The views expressed in this publication are those of the author alone and should not be taken as expert instruction or commands. While all attempts have been made to verify the information provided in this publication, neither the author nor the publisher assumes any responsibility for errors, omissions, or contrary interpretation of the subject matter herein.

Printed and bound in India

For Sale in Indian Subcontinent Only

This book is dedicated to all the people
going to work every day to make someone else rich.

Now it's your turn.

Contents

Disclaimer: I'm not an attorney or an accountant. I give advice based on my experiences and successes. I don't claim anything in this book to be legal advice, estate advice, or tax advice. Please check with your attorney or accountant before using any of the techniques discussed in this book. All investing strategies have inherent risks and should not be taken lightly. Any claims in this book are my results and/or the stated results of students. Your results may differ. Results are not guaranteed.

Acknowledgments

I wish to thank all the people who have attended my classes, seminars, and masterminds. Your kind words, encouragement, and 5-star reviews have made it easy for me to keep going, even when I am tired or unmotivated. You all are my inspiration.

I would like to also recognize the people who are or have worked for Investor Schooling. Phil Falcone my partner, Jamie Lenegan our senior Student Liaison, Paul Marturano our marketing director, Ken McArthur our assistant producer, Pedro Quinones our show and studio producer, and all the others who helped along the way, such as Fred Posimo, Evan Zaremba, Carrie Smith, Stone Falcone, and so many more.

Mostly, I would like to recognize my wife, Linda Steinhouse, who has to put up with my crap at home and at work!

Thanks to all of you!

Foreword

Have you ever watched those late-night infomercials? The ones where motivational speakers are trying to convince you that you're just three easy payments away from completely changing your life and receiving the wealth of your dreams? Better yet, have you ever made one of those late-night purchases? If you have, there's a really good chance you still have that binder of "life-changing material" sitting under your bed, covered in dust. Don't feel bad. You're in good company. That was me once upon a time. I had a whole collection of those binders.

The problem is that about 99 percent of consumers who buy those things never apply that incredible material. But I'm telling you, the problem isn't the material. It's the person holding it. Now, I'm not trying to make you feel bad or guilty about that. It's actually good news! Because you're also the solution.

Right now, you're holding this book in your hands, and what you do next is going to be the beginning of the next chapter in your life. Now, you might have the passion—you might be pretty fired up about everything that Larry has laid out for you in these pages—but I'm telling you right now that passion alone isn't going to produce the alchemy you're looking for. No, true success takes more than that. In my book *Think and Grow Rich: Three Feet from Gold*, I talk about the Success Equation, which gives you the blueprint for true success. According to that equation, you need to add to your passion talent and know-how, put the principles of this book into action, keep an association with like-minded people, and maintain your faith that you're on the right the right track.

And by opening this book, you *are* on the right track.

How do I know this? Well, I've known Larry for a long time. He is the embodiment of the Success Equation. And trust me, I know it when I see it. I have had the very unique opportunity of sitting down with greats such as the guy who invented string theory, the president of NASA, the founder of the Make a Wish Foundation, and the gentleman building the elevator to space. There is a fabric in all of them that has taken them to the heights where they are today. It isn't hard to spot those commonalities, and I can see them in Larry, too. Now, I don't know about you, but that is enough to make me want to pay attention to what he has to say.

The last thing I need to say here is that when you start living in the Success Equation and you commit to applying the financial strategies, you're going to learn here in this book, there will be some nay-sayers in your life. Some days, the loudest one might be you. Change can be hard. Adopting new ideas and practices can be uncomfortable. Napoleon Hill, the author of *Think and Grow Rich*, once wrote, "You have no idea what it's like when not a soul on earth encourages you and all the negative forces pour in. It takes super-human strength and will to throw them off. I'd give anything if I had someone tell me I can succeed, even if they didn't believe it themselves."

Well, I'm here to tell you that you can succeed. Success is a choice. When you know in your heart you're doing something right and you're on the right path, don't ever let other people talk you out of your dream. Always seek the counsel, ignore the opinion, and never throw in the towel. Today, you are three feet from the gold. Now I challenge you to turn the page and close that gap.

Best of luck and keep smiling.

Greg Reid
Speaker, Author, Filmmaker

Instructions for This Book

Before you get into everything I'm going to share with you here, I need you to make a deal with me: Don't just read this book then walk away like you do with almost every other book you've ever read. Because I know what's going to happen. You're going to start reading this book and you're going to be blown away by everything you're learning. You're going to make promises to yourself that you're going to start implementing these strategies and you're going to daydream about all the money you're going to make when you do.

But here's the thing. As soon as you close the book, your regular life is going to be there staring you in the face. Maybe there's a load of laundry that needs to be switched over or there are calls you have to make or an appointment you have to get to. Whatever it is, it's going to feel a lot more demanding than something you read in a book once—regardless of how mind-blowing it was.

So, I'm going to give you a blueprint on exactly how to use this book so that you actually use this book:

> **Mess it up:** Underline everything you want to remember. Write in the margins. Use a highlighter. Make this book yours. If it's something you read and decide you want to share with someone, buy them their own copy. When you use the book like this, it deepens your engagement and helps you remember more of what you're reading.
>
> **Use sticky notes:** Do yourself a favor and don't turn another page before you go and get a stack of sticky notes to keep next to you. Flag the action items you are committed to doing and the things you want to come back to.
>
> **Set goals:** Better yet, write down a deadline on those sticky notes before you put them in your book. Set goals and make commitments as you go.
>
> **Read it again:** I promise you, there are things you're going to forget and there are things that maybe you're not ready to hear today but the next time you read it you will be. That's why it's important that you read this book more than once. Today, maybe you're just worried about fixing your credit. But a year from now—especially if you've been using the strategies I'm giving you—you might be a lot more interested in how to avoid paying tens of thousands of dollars in taxes or how to buy houses using other people's money.

Whatever you do, don't just treat this like a book.

It's not supposed to be.

Introduction

Many people talk about the big "why" in their lives. They often refer to their children or their spouse and say, "I'm doing it for them!" I have found this to be a big crock of crap. If your "why" doesn't have you in it, it isn't a why—it's more of a righteous statement. When I drill down my clients further for a big why, they go to the next obvious answer: I want a better life! Oy, this is another crock! Until you have a real why—something you are deeply passionate about—you will never really head towards your goal or the life you desire.

I have created and planned my life in every step, and I am reaping the rewards every day. Wanna know my why?

I'm dying.

Did you feel a little flutter in your heart when you read that sentence? Well, it's not just me—you are dying, too! That's right. Every day you get closer to death, and nothing can stop that. It's true—we are all dying. We're all here on borrowed time. But it's the flutter and concern you felt when you read the first sentence that told you the real truth. You see, when I say we're all dying, you may just roll your eyes, thinking *I know, I know, Larry!* I wonder, though, if the magnitude of that fact really hits home for you. Do you feel the weight of it sometimes? I hope so. Because understanding that fact can be a real motivator.

Imagine going to the doctor today and hearing those words: You're dying. You have only a certain amount of time to live.

What would be your first reaction? What would you want to do most in all the world?

You would want to live!

I wish that for you right now. Imagine how your life would be if you were ignited by that kind of passion for living. You would truly live every single day of this borrowed time. That passion to live—before it's too late—is my why. It is what drives me to keep reaching for my dreams.

When you have a dream, you have exactly two choices: You can let it die, or you can live the dream. I will tell you that when your dreams die, you die; when your dreams live, you live.

For most Americans, every day is the same old tired routine: Get up, take a shower, eat breakfast, get in the car, go to work, get a paycheck, struggle to pay bills, rinse, and repeat.

This is called "making a living."

It is a recipe for death.

It's no wonder that our society is plagued with stress, heart attacks, and depression. That tired routine is no way to make the complex human organism happy! We are created with desires and dreams that need to be fulfilled. Is your dream to work for someone else? Do you want to be owned by your employer or a faceless company—little more than a slave? Do you want to be a mouse in a maze, forever traveling the same road to the same destination, getting the same piece of cheese—a paycheck—at the end of every week?

No!

If you're trapped in this maze, my guess is that you are under the delusion that your dreams have no value. You are afraid.

Let this be the moment that you decide to let all of that go. Let this be the moment in your life that you can look back on and say, "That's when I decided to try another way."

I've decided I'm going to live every dream I have before I die. Why? Because I don't know what happens to me after that. No one does. I hope it's what my minister says—I hope I go to Heaven and it's going to be a party with God and Jesus. I hope all that stuff is going to be exactly as I've heard it's supposed to be. But either way, it doesn't matter. Not to my dreams, anyway. Whether it's true or not true—once I pass the finish line, whatever is happening here doesn't matter anymore. This moment we have to live—right here, the way we want to—will be gone forever.

So, live! Have a blast!

My Why

The number one thing I enjoy most is helping other people. Second to that is making money. Luckily, I figured out a way to help people and to make money doing it. My school for investor students, Investor Schooling, is a true two-in-one deal. When I teach, I touch lives. In some ways, maybe it's a bit selfish of me to want to help so many people. To me, helping others is the ultimate experience in living; and in living, I get to do something for myself. But honestly, those two whys are not really that far apart at all. I mean, the best and fastest way that you can do your part to change the world is to make money.

Let that sink in for a moment.

It's really true. How many times have you wanted to donate to another country? How many times have you wanted to donate to a cause that was important to you? How many times have you wished you could quit your job and spend the rest of your life serving somewhere? When you are making enough money, you can do all those things. You really can make the world better by making money. We have all heard the analogy of putting your oxygen mask on first before helping another person put on an oxygen mask. It's the same with money. If you're making money, you can control the flow of those blessings elsewhere—but first you have to have them in your possession.

That's why I wrote this book. I wrote this book to help as many people as I can to understand money and how it really works—and then they, in turn, can go out and do their parts to change the world faster. And trust me—there are a lot of people out there who don't know how money works. Even people who think they get it often do not get it. It's kind of like learning a language. You can see it with kids. They start talking and it's just a few words here and there. By the time they're ready to start school, they are considered fluent, but they still don't have the same command of the language as an adult does. That's going to take many more years of maturity and practice. At that point, it's not just about being fluent in the language—it's being able to use the language to fully express yourself. It becomes something else entirely than just a list of words.

Money is the same way. Even if you think you're managing it well or that you're adequately getting things set up for your future, I promise you there is still a world of things you don't know that you don't know. And unfortunately, maturity and practice aren't going to naturally teach you these things. Most people don't know the things I'm going to tell you. But once you know them, your understanding of money will allow you to use money in a completely different way. You will be able to use money to express your desires in a way that makes them realities. Your goals may not change, but you're going to be able to meet them a heck of a lot easier and faster.

In This Book

I'm going to teach you how money can make money. I want to convince you not to be afraid to borrow money to make money. That's how confident you will be in these strategies. You'll be so positive you know how to do it right that you won't dare miss that opportunity. You're also going to know how to lend money to make money. I'm going to give you fail-safe strategies for that, too. You won't be afraid to let your money go because you'll be certain that it will come back to you at a profit. I'm going to teach you the truth about your credit score, how to rebuild your credit using credit cards, how to make money in a bad economy, how to use your every-day expenses to help build your credit and increase your income, and so much more.

When you reach this kind of fluency in money, you will be financially safer than you've ever been. You will be recession proof. You won't have to count on anyone else for money ever again—not even the government. Is Social Security going to go away? Maybe—but you won't care about that anymore. It will just be a bonus check if it's still around by the time you're eligible for it. You won't have to worry about the government changing its tax laws anymore. The rich do pay taxes, but I'm going to show you how they pay less taxes because of what they know—and it's all completely legal.

The 3 Stages of Learning

This book is going to make you get out of your comfort zone. I've learned that learning something new has three stages. The first stage is "Huh?" I'm going to teach you things that blow your mind and go against everything you've ever learned about money. This is going to be a little uncomfortable for you because it's going to force you to accept that the things you've been taught may not, in fact, be true.

The next stage of learning is "Hmm . . ." I'm going to make a case for what I'm teaching you. I'm going to show you evidence and give you the data you need in order to see that what I'm telling you is true. You're going to give yourself permission to consider what I'm saying—to accept that it is not the ranting of a mad man—and to consider that what has worked for me and countless others could possibly work for you, too.

The final stage of learning is "Ah!" There will be a lightning bolt of understanding. You will see exactly how to implement the strategies I'm giving you. You won't be able to wait to go out there and try them. You will want to hit the ground running.

Knowledge is power. And in this case, it's also money. It's time for you to learn these money secrets and put them into practice. If this book proves to be the vehicle that takes you where you want to go, then thank you. If my living out my why somehow influences you to live out yours, then we become legends together.

And that's more than enough living for me.

CHAPTER 1

Money Mindset

I want you to clear your mind and take a deep breath. I'm going to give you a word to think about, and I want you to pay attention to your reaction to this word. The word is . . . money.

What was your gut reaction to the word? Honestly? You may have felt a thrill go through your whole body. Or maybe you felt anxiety. Maybe you felt uncertainty. It's possible that you felt peace. Whatever it was, I want you to sit with the truth of that feeling and hold on to that as we dig deeper into this chapter.

Myth vs. Truth

The feelings you felt come from your money mindset. Now, money itself is a neutral thing. But we attach all kinds of ideas to it and call them "truth." But are they? For example, here are just a few myths you might believe about money, and I want you to notice how they make you feel:

1. *Money doesn't grow on trees*
   This is the idea that you don't have an endless supply of money. But that doesn't have to be true. If it is, that just means you bought the wrong tree.
2. *Money is the root of all evil*
   First of all, this line is misquoted. The actual quote is, "The *love of money* is the root of all evil." It's from the Bible. What it's actually saying is that you shouldn't love money more than you love God. I agree, but it doesn't mean you can't enjoy and love your money. Just don't make the mistake of putting money number one in your life. Money itself is not evil. It's a neutral thing. It's how you perceive money or what you do with it that gives it a value.
3. *Families get torn apart by money*
   If you believe that families get torn apart by money, you aren't going to have any money. You simply will not allow it to flow into your life. But is it true that money will destroy your most important relationships like that? No. Families get torn apart by selfishness and greed—not money. If your family is selfish and greedy, it doesn't matter if you have a million dollars or two dollars. The attitudes will be the same.
4. *You should never discuss money with your children*
   That is a mistake. If you have children, start discussing money with them right now. I have a business partner who started putting credit cards in his son's name several years

ago. When his son turned 18 years old, he had an 850 credit score. The world is his oyster. It's brilliant.

Master or Slave?

These are just some of the many myths out there about money. The ones you believe and buy into are the ones that control your relationship with money. Are you the master or the slave? If you're not sure, answer this question: Are you stressed over any of your financial obligations? If so, money is mastering you. And that is a choice. If you want to be a master of money, don't stress over your bills. Who cares? Your phone could be ringing from bill collectors all day long, your bank account could be empty—and it's still a choice whether or not you're going to stress over that. And as soon as you give yourself up to the stress and the worry and the fear, you are a slave.

Instead of living in fear of money, live in expectation and gratitude of money. This one change in your mindset will multiply it faster than you can imagine.

In his book *Secrets of the Millionaire Mind*, T. Harv Ecker talks about picking up pennies when he finds them. How many people would pick up a penny if they saw it on the street (even when it isn't heads up)? I would imagine that not many people would do that. But T. Harv Ecker says that if you don't pick up the change on the street, then you aren't receiving the gift that was put in your path. And if God puts a penny in your path and you refuse it by not picking it up, why would He give you a nickel, a dime, or a dollar?

Always remember that every set of 100 pennies is a dollar that can go to work for you, never asking for a day off or calling in sick. If you kick it to the side, it will go work for someone else who is willing to pick it up. Make sure you treat it with the respect it deserves!

This might sound silly to you, but I'm being serious. Start picking up pennies if you see them on the street. When you do this, strange things are going to happen. Money is going to start flowing into your life. I promise you it will. I once had a protégé who I challenged to start picking up pennies when she found them. She was a single mom with three children, and she was struggling to pay her bills. Shortly after she started picking up pennies, she found a $10 bill in the street. Then one day all these things started to happen in her financial life; it completely changed. It wasn't long before she did her first real estate deal, and she made more money in that transaction than she made in almost half a year in her job. And then, would you believe it, she ended up marrying a rich, handsome man. It was me! That student is now my wife.

Don't Let Your Mindset Hold You Back

When you change your mindset, you will have power over money instead of the other way around. This is a universal truth—it doesn't just apply to money. The only thing that can ever hold you back from doing what you have always wanted to do is you. Granted, there are times when people may have a disability or something that is serious that really can hold them back, but it doesn't hold them back to the point where they cannot do anything. The only thing that holds you back is your own mind.

For instance, I have a rare genetic disorder called Gaucher disease. There are three types of Gaucher disease. One type causes children who are born with it to, most often, pass away before they are five years old. Another type allows children to possibly live into their teens, but they will have severe brain damage. Luckily, I have the livable type of the disease, but it still comes with some serious problems. It eats organs and bones, which are very helpful to, you know, surviving. The other thing it does is that it makes people extremely tired at times. I take treatment for the disease, and I'm living a pretty good life in spite of my diagnosis.

There is a two-hour treatment I take every two weeks. There used to be just one factory that made the enzyme for this treatment. Well, that factory got a virus. Millions of patients could no longer get their treatments. They asked for volunteers who would be willing to skip their treatments for a while. I volunteered. It took almost three years before I started getting tired, whereas other volunteers were bed ridden after a week without treatment. These are people with the exact same disease and type of the disease that I have. We have the same prognosis, the same odds stacked against us. So, what gives? Why wasn't I in bed after a few days? I'm telling you, the biggest difference between me and those other volunteers was our mindset. I have Gaucher disease, but I refuse to *be* Gaucher disease.

Lean In

When we fear something, it has more power over us. I learned a powerful lesson about this years ago, and it was a lesson I'll never forget. At the time, I was learning Karate. I was sparring, and my opponent, who was better than me, would throw a kick or punch. I kept side-stepping his blows. But I quickly found that if I stepped back, he was able to hit me a lot harder than if I stayed where I was. By moving away, I gave him the opportunity to fully extend his leg or his arm, which made the impact more powerful. So, I started to step in instead. And I found that he couldn't hit me anymore. Not only did I keep him from fully extending, but as I stepped in, he would step back. Now who was afraid?

This principle changed my life. There are times I get up in the morning and I don't want to get out of bed. Those are the days I get out of bed faster, and I encourage you to do this. If you are having a bad day, step in—don't step back. Make that extra phone call, go see that extra person, send that extra piece of mail. Do whatever you need to do to make your business better.

Think and Grow Rich

There's a book called *Think and Grow Rich*. It is the product of many interviews the author, Napoleon Hill, conducted over many years. He went out and started interviewing millionaires, but this was back in the 30s, so they would have been billionaires by today's standards. The basis of his questions revolved around one burning question: what is the secret to getting rich? To his surprise, he found a common thread through all of the answers. All of those wealthy men talked about how they had first wished for something or thought really hard about something, and then that wish or thought materialized. And they didn't just think about it—they were consumed by their burning desires for those things.

I can relate. You see, the only reason I have a school filled with students is because I first had a burning desire to open a school. There were a lot of times I doubted myself because I wasn't sure how I would get students, or I wasn't sure I would have enough material to teach them. But I had the *desire*. Napoleon Hill talks about that in his book and says that God—or the Universe, or whatever it is you believe in—will put everything in your way to make the desires of your heart happen. You may not actually know how those things get in your path, but they get there. My school is a living testament to that truth. Literally, what you get is what you've imagined.

Back in 2008, I filed bankruptcy, but I didn't stay down very long. I didn't spend time feeling sorry for myself. I spent my time creating the next chapter of my life, and I knew that began by seeing it. So, I imagined that I was going to come out of bankruptcy and rebuild everything and become a millionaire again. And I've done it. It was not a fluke. I did it very intentionally, beginning the day I left bankruptcy court. Today, my credit score routinely goes as high as 800 and my net worth is over a million dollars. I am on track to hit my next milestone of having a net worth of $5 million, and I know I will get there because I already see it.

You literally get where you imagine. So, here is the really important question: What do you imagine? Do you imagine problems, or do you imagine solutions? Do you spend your time thinking about the misery of the life you're living, or are you focusing your thoughts on building the life that you want?

Someone once told me to write a check to myself for the amount of money I want to have in twenty years. I did it, and I encourage you to do the same. Write that check. Make it as big as you can dream it to be. Date it for the goal date—the date you plan on being able to cash that check. And then put that check in your wallet. Keep it close to you. If you don't have a check, then write it on a slip of paper. Either way, I want you to write it down. You've thought it, you've written it—you have already started the creation process. Do you understand? There are a finite number of steps between you and that dollar amount. By thinking it and by writing it down, you have now taken the first two steps. That shows God that you are ready for the next step, the next door to open.

That is how you create a life your future self will be proud of.

Counterfactual Simulation

Once you shift your mindset and you have planted your desire, the pathway there will manifest itself—but you need to do your part to help that along. I have a friend who is a billionaire. His name is Brian, and he is also my coach. He told me about something that changed my life. It's called counterfactual simulation.

A counterfactual simulation is the process of letting your mind explore the "what ifs." You make the assumption that something is already true and suspend your disbelief. You give your imagination the space to roam free and simulate all the "what ifs" that would make your dream a reality. And then you can identify all the doors that have to open in order for you to get there. Those doors may sound impossible and far-fetched, but you allow yourself to mentally walk through them and explore the possibilities. The idea is that you see the reality that you want, and then basically reverse engineer it.

For instance, let's say you want to have an additional $1.25 million sitting in your bank account five years from now. You would begin by believing it is true. Then you would ask yourself, "What needs to happen between now and then for that to happen?" You would begin by looking at where you're starting today. Let's say you have $20,000 in your account right now. In simple terms, you would have to put away $250,000 a year for the next five years. That breaks down to $21,000 a month, or $695 a day. Now, what would you have to do to earn that money? This will move you into another set of simulations. What if you invested that $20,000 into real estate? How could that snowball into $695 a day or $250,000 a year for the next five years? Go down those roads. Ask those questions and let your imagination answer them.

When I first heard of this, I thought it was both crazy and amazing at the same time.

Now I want you to get a piece of paper and a pen and do this. Take just five minutes and write down where you want to be in five years. If there is a certain dollar amount you want to have or a number of houses you want to own, write those down. Whatever your goals are for five years from now, write them down. Do your own counterfactual simulation and allow yourself to believe you're there and to see the path of how to get there. In this practice, anything is possible. Let your imagination run free!

Dare to believe that the impossible can happen. You will discover that anything is possible!

The Impossible *Can* Happen

One time, I was just sitting in a parking lot doing some work on my phone when a woman saw my truck and knocked on the window. I rolled down the window, and she asked, "Do you guys buy office condos?" I said yes, so she took my number and said she'd call me to set up a time for me to see her office.

When she called to set things up, before I even saw the office, she told me, "The best office in the complex has already sold for $150,000. I don't want that much, but I do have a bottom-line number." I told her no problem, and I went to see the space.

The space was perfect. I figured her bottom-line was probably going to be $100,000, but I was not going to offer that right out of the gate. I took my time to look around as I was formulating my plan. Finally, I asked, "Do you need the money?"

"No," she said. "My husband is a doctor. We just want out. But we're not looking for a low-ball."

I nodded. "Okay. Tell you what. I will give you $500 a month for 100 months and a $50,000 balloon payment at the end."

That was a ludicrous offer. But she was silent for a minute as she calculated everything in her head. Then a big smile broke across her face. "Deal," she said.

Now, you're probably thinking, *Larry, that still comes to $100,000, and you said you were going to offer less!*

Well, consider this: How many people have a $500 car loan? I have a condo payment that's $500, and it is 100 percent principal. I am paying 0 percent in interest. Heck yeah, I saved money. And remember—the property is valued at about $150,000 and I can rent that place for $1,900 a month. I came out way ahead. It's all about mindset. First, you have to shift yourself in order to believe the impossible is possible. Then, you will discover that it is.

Three Feet from Gold

There is a story in *Think and Grow Rich* called "Three Feet from Gold." The story goes like this: There was a guy who was mining for gold. Early on, he found some gold. But after a few loads of ore, the vein of gold seemed to end. He kept digging for many months but only came up empty. Finally, he concluded that he had found all there was to find on that piece of land, so he sold all of his mining equipment to a "junk dealer" and quit. However, the dealer who had bought the equipment was a pretty smart guy. He hired a mining engineer. The engineer told him exactly where to dig, and the guy found a vein of gold just three feet from where the first guy had stopped digging. He made millions.

How many times have you been three feet from gold? I know I have been there a lot. In fact, I have a daily reminder on my phone that says, "You are three feet from gold."

A few years ago, I bought some office space. I did seller financing, and I put about $10,000 into it to give it some upgrades, and I expected I could rent it for about $4,000 a month. It was beautiful. I put it up for rent, and there were no takers. After six months, I brought the price down and put it up for $3,600 a month. Three months later, I dropped it to $3,000. Then for $2,300. After that, I was desperate to have someone—anyone—to rent it. I was willing to rent it for $2,000—a negative cashflow—just to stop the bleeding.

But guess what? The reason it wasn't renting was because I was supposed to take it. I just didn't know it yet. That space is where I now have my school, Investor Schooling. Luckily, I held onto it long enough for that to be a possibility. You see, that space could have been a bad deal. I could have given up on it all together just to get out of it. But I didn't. I held onto it and waited for time to close the gap between what I thought it was supposed to be and what it was actually supposed to be. Three feet from gold.

As you work on your money mindset, will you be positive all the time? No, it's impossible. We all have our bad days. But the more and more you stack up those good days, the more powerful your positive mindset will become. You will be an unstoppable force as the creator of your own destiny.

CHAPTER 2

What Is Money Anyway?

It is amazing to me that something as important as money is so misunderstood. I don't want to bore you with the unimportant details of money, but like every troubled child, money had troubled beginnings. So, let's talk about what it was supposed to be, what it actually is, and why it's important for you to look at it in a whole new way.

The Gold Standard

Money is simply pieces of paper or trinket-size coins that we exchange for goods and wares. Sounds simple, doesn't it? Well, as you have already surmised, it is not simple at all.

There was a time when money was equal to a value of gold. Simply put, your certificate or dollar was equal to a specific amount of gold. That meant that when you acquired money, it was considered to be a receipt for the corresponding piece of gold of equal value held in a safe place, such as the Federal Reserve. While you held that dollar or "gold certificate," you laid claim to or "owned" that piece of gold. Therefore, the total amount of money in circulation was equal to the amount of gold being held in reserve.

You may be asking, "Why use money at all, then? Why not just use gold?" Well, the answer is simple. Using the notes was a lot more reliable. If gold were valued by weight, then on which scale should or would it be measured? If you went into a car dealer to buy a $60,000 car, then you would need about two pounds of gold (assuming gold was worth about $1,800/ounce, as it is in today's market). If your scale said it was 2 pounds and the dealer's scale said it was 1.93 pounds . . . well, you can quickly understand the problems with that scenario. So, the dollar was more reliable and much more convenient. It was also much easier to carry around. Can you imagine having to carry those two pounds of gold in your pocket?

It is also important to understand that the gold standard kept all money equal in basis around the world. Everyone using the gold standard knew exactly how much gold they could lay claim to by a standard conversion figure. That conversion was simply the amount of gold that it was equivalent to. Those here in the United States converted it into dollars while other countries called the notes different things—such as marks or pounds or francs—but they all meant the same thing. They were an equivalent of the amount of gold held by the various governments.

Now, I need to emphasize the word *were*. Past tense. This is not how things are done anymore.

So, what happened to the gold standard?

Remember the Great Depression? In 1933, at the height of the Great Depression, the new president, Franklin D. Roosevelt, made the historical decision to go off of the gold standard. He raised the price of gold substantially, which meant the money in circulation at the time no longer had a one-to-one value with gold. It was deflated by about 40 percent. Furthermore, the United States had hoarded the gold supply during the Great Depression, which constricted its circulation in the world economy. It wasn't long before other countries based the value of their currencies not on gold but on the American dollar. Thus, the gold standard was no more. In fact, today sometimes a dollar is worth more than its gold equivalent and other times it is worth less. There is no calculated correlation between their values. Gold is simply a commodity like other collectables.

So, where does that leave money? Today, money and its equivalent value is arbitrary. It is now . . . paper and bits of metal. It is WORTHLESS!

Or is it?

Well, the real point I'm trying to make here is that it's important for you to look at money in a new way. Because ultimately, you and I both know that I can tell you it's worthless all day long but it doesn't change the fact that the more you have, the better it feels. You can get stuff done with some money! Personally, I am a big fan of money, and it is my goal to accumulate and circulate as much as possible.

But if it's not beholden to the gold standard, how can we possibly calculate its true value? What is it really worth?

The Time Standard

I submit to you that the real value of money is based on the "time standard."

Time can easily be translated into its hourly equivalent. Simply put, it is like an hourly wage. As an exercise, I challenge you to determine what your hourly worth is. Some people make money on an hourly basis, and it makes sense to just use that figure. For example, if you are working at a grocery store and your hourly wage is $12 an hour, then that is a good figure to use for your current hourly worth. If you're on a salary or working for fixed wages, do the math to convert your income rate to your average hourly rate. To do this, simply divide the number of actual annual working hours that you normally work into your salary. If you are a commission salesperson or work with bonuses, simply take your expected commission or bonus for the year and use the same division.

Whatever your hourly worth is, it's important to know the rate for which you are currently working and to be aware of that rate at all times. You must understand that time is money and money is time. If your hourly wage is unknown, how do you know how much money you could make if you worked a few more hours? Or how much money you are giving up by working a few hours less?

Let's say you want a new car and the new payment will be $150 more than your old payment. How much of your life is that going to cost you? If your hourly worth is $15 an hour, it will cost you an extra ten hours every month. If your hourly value is $50 an hour, it will cost you three. But it doesn't stop there. If you're financing the vehicle, then part of that $150 is interest. That means you're not just working for extra bells and whistles on the car—you're also working for the "privilege" of being able to work longer for them! Is all of that extra time investment worth the advantages of the new car? Well, maybe. But it depends on your hourly worth.

The monetary experts talk about the dollar as its buying power compared to each country. They compare how much a US dollar will buy compared to another country's currency. If you understand this, then you understand that each and every person or family has their own micro economy within their own household as it relates to hours worked. The monetary cost of an item is fixed for both the high earner as well as the low earners. If a car is priced for $30,000, it will be $30,000 for someone who makes $50 an hour and someone who makes $15 an hour. The number of hours each of these people have to work for that car, however, is drastically different. In that way, the actual cost of the car is different from person to person. Therefore, you need to compare the cost of your purchases to your own internal economy—not the world's external economy.

Consider that the average car payment for an average car is about $340 per month for five years. That means that if you make $40,000 per year, you are currently working twenty hours—or half a work week—each month to pay for your car. Okay, that might not sound that bad to you if you're picturing the car you want for that $340. But now think of it this way: don't think about that car. Instead, imagine your boss comes in and says to you, "I need you to work an extra twenty a month for the next five years. But don't worry, we will give you a company vehicle to use however you want." What is the first thought that comes to your mind? Better yet, what is the first feeling? Does it feel like a pretty good deal? Does it feel like you just lost twenty hours of your life each month? Are you thinking of all the things you had planned on doing instead?

Don't think in terms of things. Think in terms of time. What does that mean? To alter a great cliché, "Don't spend the dime if you can't do the time!"

Time is Money

I make these points because of the way I see people treating money. They simply have no respect for it. They throw it away like toilet paper in the wind—a new oversized house, a new oversized TV, a new oversized car, and so on and so on. They see something and they want it, end of story. They don't usually think of the true cost of those things. They are literally exchanging pieces of their lives for those material possessions. If we exchanged real gold for our possessions, we might feel the impact of our purchases more. Imagine again plopping down two pounds of real gold to buy a car. It sounds ludicrous, but maybe if you did that, the impact of your purchase would be understood a little better.

I want you to think about your hourly worth—the time standard of your money—and relate it to everything you're exchanging money for in your life. Don't think in terms of the amount of dollars things will cost you anymore—think in terms of the amount of time things will cost you. If you consider the time conversion very carefully with everything you purchase or invest in, your life will change.

When you're considering a purchase, ask yourself, "How many hours of work will that item cost me?" I will tell you now that when you start to think this way, your entire outlook will change. You will spend differently. You will work differently. You will invest differently. You will live differently.

For instance, let's say you find out the local golf club is having a half-day special and you can "save today if you play today." Normally it's $60 to play, but today it is $30. You think, *Wow—a big $30 savings!* and you decide to take the day off of work so that you can spend your time on the golf course.

Well, let's examine the true cost of your round of golf: If you've calculated your hourly worth to be, say, $30 an hour and you normally work an eight-hour day, you've already spent $240 in lost wages on that game. You saved $30 because of the special, but it still cost you $30 to play. That brings the total cost of your golf outing to $270. It will take you nine hours of your life to recover that investment—and that doesn't even take into account your other incidentals, such as lunch, drinks, or balls lost, which may be the cash equivalent to another hour or two of your time.

How about that big screen HDTV that costs you $3,000? The true cost, based on the example of your hourly worth being $30 an hour, is 100 hours of your life.

Remodeling your kitchen for $12,000? That will cost you 400 hours of your life (and that's assuming you hire someone else to do all the work for you and aren't putting any hours in yourself).

Grabbing a $4 gourmet coffee on your way to work every morning? That will cost you about 35 hours over the course of one year, which is about an entire week of work.

Spending $90 a month on a gym membership you never use? That will cost you another week of work over the course of a year.

You should clearly think about each and every purchase this way. How many hours will it take to buy something? Remember, your time is finite! Everything you invest your time/money in also comes with an opportunity cost. What could you have spent that time/money on instead?

Money Makes Money

So, now that we've established that you work for things—not money—over time, it's also important to understand the flip side of that. If invested wisely, money can work for you and it can make you money over time.

Time after time we are told about the compound features of money, but many people do not fully understand the impact of that principle. One of my heroes, P. T. Barnum, once said something along the lines of, "People can't work on Sundays, but money can." This is a great quote! It simply means that money has the ability to gain interest every day. It does not take a holiday or a sick day. Even when the banks are closed, the bank is paying (or charging) daily interest on your money.

So, what does this mean?

Let's examine this idea for a minute. Imagine there is a fortune teller whose every prediction has always come true. She can give you years and years and years of proof of this. So, you decide to go to her for your fortune. She tells you that your newborn son is guaranteed to win the $1-million lottery by the time he reaches the age of 65. The fortune teller cannot tell you the exact day, but she says you must play the lottery for the child every day, for if you miss even one day, you are sure to have those numbers come up on that day—the day you do not play. And remember, this fortune teller is never wrong! So, what would you do? Would you say, "Oh, that's too much of a hassle!" and decide not to do it? Or would you play the lottery every day, even if it meant you might have to play every single day for the next 65 years?

I hope the answer is obvious. We're talking about *a million dollars*.

So, if you would do that, then think about this: If you were to start an investment account for your child the year he was born and put in a dollar a day, 365 days a year, every year for 65 years—with an investment interest rate of about 8.5 percent—he would have over $1 million in that account by his 65th birthday. To really understand how significant that is, it's important to point out that you would have only deposited $23,725 into that account over his entire lifetime. The interest made by that "hardworking" money would be over $975,000.

Now let's say you calculated your hourly worth to be $30 an hour. How long would it take you to make that amount of money? You would have to work 32,500 hours, which comes to 813 forty-hour work weeks, which comes to 15.6 years of working Monday through Friday without any vacation days.

Save Your Time, Invest Your Money!

Now, you may be thinking that all sounds pretty good, but where will you get the extra money to invest? Ah, now that is a good question.

The *first* answer I will give you is to go back and consider all the other areas in your life where you are spending your time—er, your money—that could be invested more wisely.

I recently read the Warren Buffett biography *Snowball* and was amazed that far into Mr. Buffet's accumulation of money, his wife, Suzy, was cutting coupons and saving pennies for everyday items. Now remember, Warren Buffett was at times the richest man in America, and his wife was using coupons!

When you purchase something, it is good to shop around to get the best price. I have found through the years that shopping for something secondhand from websites like eBay has saved me thousands. Most of the time, you can find the exact item that you are looking for in perfect condition, or even brand new, for huge discounts. Sometimes it even has the manufacturer's warranty along with it. Imagine if you could work only 100 hours for that HDTV instead of 147 hours. That is a lot of hours saved. The newness wears off pretty quickly anyway, and it becomes a used item to you as soon as you turn it on for the first time. In the case of a car, you could save thousands by buying a used car instead of a showroom new car. The only difference will be that you will get the car with that first ding already in it. On average, a two-year-old car costs about 40 percent less than the original sticker price. Now that is a bargain!

And the *second* answer I will give you is this: Keep reading this book and find out!

CHAPTER 3

How Much Money Do You Want?

I want to talk to you a little bit about what you want out of life—out of your goals—and, honestly, why most of us are stuck.

If you're reading this book, I'm going to assume that you'd like more money. But, how much more money? If you don't know, then I could hand you a dollar bill and *Poof!* you'd have more money. So, you would have achieved your goal, right?

No, Larry! I want more money than that. Money through the roof!

Okay, great. Let me take a big bag of pennies and start stacking them, one on top of the other, until they're literally going through the roof. *Poof!* Money going through the roof. You're welcome.

I hope you understand the problem here. If you're not specific in asking for what you want, then how can you get it?

But here's the crazy part: I guarantee you that you are already getting everything that you want. You might be thinking, *That doesn't make any sense, Larry! I'm broke! I'm trying to learn to invest so I can get out of the rat race, but until then, I'm stuck. How can you say that I have everything I want?*

I can say it because it's true. What you have right now is what you've created for yourself. Your life is a manifestation of exactly what you have pursued, purchased, and created—with your time, your desires, your money, and your life. Until you change the schematics of what you want—what you *really* want—in your mind, you're not going to get anything different than what you have. If you keep getting the same results in your life, it's because you're doing the same thing over and over again. Change what you're doing, and your results will change.

I have a very respected coach and friend who is really deep into the Law of Attraction. One day he came to me with a smile on his face as if he just knew he was about to change my life. He said, "Larry, take out a piece of paper. Now, write down a list of everything you like to do."

So, I started jotting down the things I love to do most—teaching, building new businesses, speaking, growing my net worth, spending time with my family, and on and on it went.

When I was done, he said, "Now look at your list and tell me everything on there that you aren't doing."

I looked at the list and laughed. "Dave, I'm doing all these things."

"Really?" he asked in disbelief. "Okay, then, what *else* would you like to do?" he asked.

I looked back down at the list and shrugged. "Honestly, I'd just like to do more of these same things."

He was impressed. Clearly, I'm part of a small minority of people who can say they are actually doing the things they want to do. My philosophy is simple: If I want to do it, I'm doing it. The trick, though, is that you have to do it on purpose. You can't just make your list or create your vision board and think you've done what it takes. The list is not the key. It's the *purpose* of the list that makes the difference, which is to keep your desires on the tip of your tongue and at the forefront of your mind, always. When you do that, it heightens your perception of the opportunities around you that will take you where you want to go. When you train your mind in such a way that you have perfect clarity on what you want, it will be easy for you to pass up the things you don't want. And trust me—your path will be full of imposter dreams.

Believing is Achieving

That's how my Corvette came into my possession. First, I decided I wanted a Corvette. I determined exactly what I wanted, then I kept visualizing it, over and over again, for the next six months. I knew it had to be a stick shift, it had to have a heads-up display—basically, it had to have all the features you can possibly get, which is the LT3 model. The problem is that it's hard to find. What happened is that I kept finding cars that were close but not quite there. This happened over and over again, and I passed on every single one of them. It didn't matter how many features it had—I could only see what was missing, and I wasn't willing to settle.

Finally, my car appeared. It was exactly what I wanted. I didn't even hesitate to buy it, despite the fact it was a little more expensive than I'd planned. I knew it was mine the minute it showed up.

Here's another example: When my wife and I were looking to buy a house, we first looked in a 55-and-older community, knowing that stage of our lives wasn't too far in the future. We found one that we really liked. We started talking about it and became more and more sold on that house, but then we said, "You know what, let's just take another look around before we decide. Let's just see what else is out there."

We started looking at other houses, and every time we opened the door on a house, we just felt *meh.* House after house was like this. Finally, we sat down and decided that the most important feature we wanted was to be able to open the door to our home and see the whole thing at first glance. We wanted to feel a sense of grandeur and openness in the floorplan. That's when we became certain about two things: one, we weren't going to buy that first house we loved in the 55-and-up community because it didn't meet those criteria; and two, we hadn't seen anything like that yet, so we had to keep looking.

Weeks went by. After looking at house after house, we find a house on the MLS listing that looked beautiful from the outside. The inside pictures were horrible, but it was in our price range and we liked the area, so we figured, *Why not?* We took the time to go see the property, and the second we opened the door, we turned to each other and said, "This is the one."

That was it!

We could see the entire layout of the house at first glance. That was *the thing* we were looking for. We didn't even need to see the rest of the house because the rest of the details were inconsequential. In fact, as we got deeper into the house, we were like, "Okay, we'll just have to take this wall down and that wall down, redo the bathrooms, update the kitchen, and . . ." The list went on and on. We ended up gutting the whole house. However, we didn't care because it didn't matter. Again, we knew it was our house the second it showed up. Everything from the price to the way it felt when we walked in—it was our *particular* dream come true.

Now, here is the crazy part. Linda told me months later that she and her daughters used to drive through that neighborhood and daydream about how great it would be to live there She didn't know it, but she was actually manifesting her future with those desires

Until you know what you want, you won't be able to pass up the things you don't want. Until you can feel and see what you want, you won't recognize it when it shows up—and you will fail to claim it.

The office building where I'm currently holding my classes was initially a property I bought to monetize. I intended to rent it out. However, as the weeks passed, it just wasn't happening. It stayed empty.

One day, I was sitting in that empty building waiting for a potential tenant to come take a look at the place. I was sitting there in an old folding chair, looking around at the walls that needed to be painted and the ugliest green carpet you've ever seen. Suddenly, this thought crossed my mind: *You know, if this office doesn't rent, I think this would be the best place to bring a bunch of real estate investors to help them learn how to invest in real estate. That would be so awesome. But I hope this guy rents this place!*

Well, the person who came that day didn't rent the office building. And it wasn't long after that when I was walking through again thinking, *Yeah, it would be cool to have a school here.*

Well, a week later, another guy came in and wanted to rent the space—for a school! He was walking through the property, and I could see him silently counting. I asked, "What are you doing?"

"I'm counting how many 18-inch-by-6-feet tables I could put in here."

I came up behind him, and then I looked, doing my own math. I started to see that office in a new light. I could see those tables. I could see those students. But they were *my* students!

Within two weeks, I owned the tables and the chairs, and the rest is history.

That story, however, begins much earlier than that. It was years and years earlier that I first spoke with Phil, my current business partner, about doing classes together. We always talked about one day teaching real estate to others. And now we are! The pieces showed up when the time was right.

When you know what you want, you're going to get it. Your knowing creates an unobstructed pathway for your dreams to follow to your doorstep.

The moments in my life when I don't know what I want are the moments when I'm stagnant. The same is true for you. If you're stuck thinking, *I wish I had more money, I wish I could do more things*, it's because you don't really know what you want. You don't know how much money you actually want, or you don't have a plan for how you're going to use that money.

So, let me help you get unstuck.

The Million-Dollar Challenge

I'm going to give you an exercise to do. Go ahead and grab a piece of paper and something to write with—you're going to need it for this, and it's important that you do it.

Now, imagine that I just handed you $1 million and told you to spend it—every dime. However, there are some catches: you can't give any of it away, and you can't invest it. This money is for purely selfish spending.

What I want you to do is set a timer for ten minutes and write down everything you would do with this money. The key is to be as specific as possible. For instance, if you're going to buy a car, you have to write down the year, the make and model, the color, and the color of the interior. If you're buying a house, you have to write down what town it's in, how many bedrooms, how many bathrooms, any special features it has. Does it have a pool? Okay, how deep is it? Does it have a fireplace? If so, what kind? What's the view like from the back porch?

I want you to really see these things and write them down.

It's also important that you don't just guess on the price tag. I want you to literally price out everything you're putting on your list. Check Amazon, Google, or wherever you can, to find the actual prices of these things. Don't just say, "I'm going to spend $50,000 on furniture." No, go to the website of your choice and start picking it out and adding up the price tags.

Now, remember that you only have a million dollars. Don't go a penny over. But I definitely want you to spend the whole amount if you can. So, where's it going to go?

You have ten minutes to make your list.

Do it now.

(Intermission Music)

So, your ten minutes is up. Did you spend your whole million? Did you at least make it to $500,000? Seven hundred and fifty thousand? How much of your time was spent writing? How much time was spent looking up prices? How much time was spent thinking about what you wanted to spend the money on in the first place?

There's no wrong answer. Don't worry if you didn't make it to a million. Most of my students don't on their first run of this. Mostly, I just want you to see where you are on this spectrum of knowing what it is you actually want.

In his book *High Performance Habits,* Brandon Bruchard talks about a study some researchers conducted on high performers. They asked different groups of people, "What is your latest dream? What are you excited about? What are you working on?" The study found that high performers answered those questions seven to nine seconds faster than the rest of the general population they studied. High performers have quicker answers because those answers are always sitting in the forefront of their minds. They have absolute clarity on those things.

When I asked my business partner, Phil, to do this "million-dollar" exercise, he did it, but he grumbled his way through the whole thing. He was thoroughly annoyed by this. The reason is because it was a complete waste of his time. He already knew where he'd spend an extra million dollars. That vision of what he wants is already looping through his mind on constant replay. No way did he need ten minutes to answer my question. He only needed the time necessary to write it down—no thinking required. This is why I have no doubt that I will be spending the weekend with him at his dream home sooner rather than later. He's already laid out the path to get it. It's on its way.

I know I'm starting to sound like a broken record here, but I really need you to internalize what I'm saying: *Until you know exactly what you want and exactly how you're going to get it, you're not going to have it.*

You can tell me you want more money all day long, but if all you need is a dollar to meet that requirement, then a dollar is all you're going to get.

When I was in Karate, my instructor taught us to visualize as part of our training. He would tell us to close our eyes and visualize the physical condition we wanted to be in. He wanted us to truly see ourselves being in great shape. He would often have us visualize ourselves doing a full split or kicking a high mark on a target.

I always visualized myself doing a round kick and striking the kicking bag as high as nose-level. When I first started, the best I could do was kick someone's ankles, so this was fairly ambitious of me. But I would sit there, day after day, and feel the rush of adrenaline moving through my body and my own physical power as I went into formation then kicked that spot, over and over again, in my mind.

After two years, I finally hit that spot.

Funny thing, though: I never hit any higher.

You will always get *exactly* what you ask for.

So, set your desires high. Have you ever heard the expression, "Reach for the stars and you may get the moon"? Don't make the mistake of setting your goals too low. Don't sell yourself short on what you could have when everything is available to you.

So, if you want more money, how much more money do you want?

Don't Just Think—*Do!*

Personally, I want a net worth of $10 million. Now, I'm not just sitting around and daydreaming about that $10 million. I also have a plan to get there, and I'm currently working that plan with the strategies and principles I'm giving you in this book.

One day, I was teaching these principles about clarity and visualization to a class of students, and afterwards, a student came up to me. She was pretty distraught. She said she used to buy into all that "mumbo jumbo" about vision boards and everything—until she made a vision board and never achieved anything that was on it.

I sat her down and said, "I hear you, but let me ask you a few questions. Tell me something that was on that vision board that you didn't get."

"There was a car I wanted."

"What kind of car?" I asked.

"I don't know. It was yellow; that's all I remember."

"You don't know what brand it was?"

"Maybe a Honda? I think?"

I nodded. "Okay, what else was on your vision board?"

"I don't know—probably some recreational things, such as vacations and expensive toys. I'm pretty sure there was a house somewhere in there."

Did she even hear what she was saying?!

"Okay," I said. "The fact that you don't remember anything that was on that board tells me that you did it exactly wrong. You did the exercise in order to do the exercise—and not in order to get those things—things you didn't really want in the first place.

"So, ironically," I continued, "you did get everything you wanted from that exercise—which was to complete the exercise. Ta da! Mission accomplished."

I pointed out that if she doesn't care enough about those things now to even remember what they were, she didn't care enough about them then to bring them into reality.

That's the thing. You can't just do the exercise to do the exercise. Take the million-dollar exercise above, for example. Finishing the exercise is not the point. It's the conversion that's important. I'm trying to convert you into a person with desire and clarity. Don't get clarity for the purpose of this exercise, or any other exercise. Get clarity for *you*.

Let's go back to my Karate example. Why was I able to finally hit that spot? Was it because I just sat around thinking about it and magically attracted the ability to do it? Absolutely not. I visualized it until it became so real to me that it was already mine. That cleared my path of obstacles—of the non-dreams—that could have taken my energy away from my goal. I didn't think about it and then turn on Netflix or go have a beer with my friends. Nor did I just go into the dojo every day and look at the spot and say, "One day . . ." No—I went to class, learning balance and stretching my muscles, practicing stamina and kicking higher and higher each day, until *boom*! There it was—the perfect round-kick precisely on that spot.

Similarly, if my student had done the exercise for the sake of re-setting her trajectory in life, she'd be driving that car, "whatever it was," and living in that house "that was probably on the board somewhere."

After our conversation, she admitted that she'd always been skeptical of visualizing and had never believed she could achieve those things by envisioning them.

So, she didn't.

Will you?

CHAPTER 4

Money: The Big, Fat Lie

If I was rich, I would be so happy!

I have heard this from so many people. They say it in passing; they say it in wishes, they even say it in prayer.

Do not believe this lie. Do not be fooled into thinking that you do not have to worry about how you should control and form your life after you reach wealth. Jim Carrey once said, "I hope everyone could get rich and famous and will have everything they ever dreamed of so they will know that it's not the answer."

If you apply all the principles and strategies I'm giving you in this book, and if you prove yourself to be an entrepreneur with drive, the world will open itself to you. Your future does not have to equal your past. Knowledge is power.

Money is power, too.

But power for the sake of power isn't going to take you very far. The real value of power is measured by what it allows you to do—it's meant to be a source of fuel.

Don't get me wrong—I'm not saying you shouldn't have money or seek to build your wealth. Please do! Apply every bit of advice I've given you. Go out there and get wealthy. I just also want you to understand that money itself is not a destination. Remember the "why" we talked about in the introduction? That why can drive you to accumulate wealth, but it should also be something to carry you farther than that. Ultimately, money should be a means to a greater destination. If money for the sake of money is your only goal, then what are you going to do with your life once you have it? You will have no purpose.

I know this from experience.

The Origin of Investor Schooling

Before I opened Investor Schooling, I was at a point where I was making plenty of money from my real estate business and trading stock options. I had everything I wanted. I didn't have to worry about paying bills. I didn't have to go into a job and report to anyone. I didn't have to do anything or be anywhere. I had basically retired.

Some people think that's the dream right there. But the reality was that I was sitting at home, bored stiff! You can only watch *Oprah* so many times. (I know she is not on TV anymore, which shows you how long I have been using the same joke.) I needed to find something to do with my time.

One day, a friend called me up and asked, "Hey, can you teach me a little bit about real estate?"

Yay! Something to do!

We met up, and I taught him a little bit about real estate. It felt good to talk with him and share my knowledge. I was pumped after our meeting. It reminded me of the passion and drive that got me into real estate in the first place. I was excited by the opportunity to watch a friend take the same journey I had.

After that experience, more and more people who wanted to learn about what I was doing kept calling me. I decided I was seriously going to start coaching people. I did it on the side for a while, and then I created a webinar to help me sell my coaching on a larger scale. I put out advertisements and videos promoting this webinar for six months before I actually launched it. The whole time I was promoting it, I was thinking, *I bet there's going to be 2,000 people in my webinar!* Why wouldn't there be? I knew my stuff and I was sharing instructions on how to make money. I figured it was a no brainer. I set up a studio in my house and bought all-new equipment and lights.

On January 16, 2017, the day finally came for me to launch my webinar. I went into my studio at 5:13 PM and turned everything on, getting ready for my 5:30 PM webinar. I was standing in the middle of the room, surrounded by screens and with all those lights shining on me, thinking, *This webinar is going to be loud, it's going to be bright, and it's going to be brilliant.*

As I "opened the doors," I saw there were just forty-seven people on the webinar. But hey, that wasn't too bad. It wasn't two thousand, but it was a room full. I did the math in my head, and if just half of the people in that "room" bought my coaching program, I was going to make an amazing ROI on my investment.

I put on my game face, and I pitched my coaching program for the very first time. I moved through my presentation, and I was feeling confident. At the end, I put up my offer on the side of the screen. My heart was racing. I couldn't wait to see how many people were going to buy my program. I waited for the rush of buyers to come in.

One person bought.

One.

My heart sunk. All I wanted to do was quit immediately. If it wasn't for that one purchase, I would have! If it wasn't for him, I would have said, "This is a complete waste of time!" That one sale, though, kept me in the game. I will always be grateful for that guy (even though he never showed up for any training).

After that, I figured it would still be worth doing if I could just sell two coaching programs a month. That would be awesome. I started selling a lot of coaching programs. The next thing you know, I'd joined forces with real estate tycoon Phil Falcone and created a company called Investor Schooling. We started teaching people about how to build wealth through real estate investments and trading stock options. Not long after that, we started doing a radio show about investing, real estate, and the stock market on a big local radio station in Philadelphia. The school just got better and better.

Today, I'm having so much fun doing these things that I don't want to stop. I often come in on my day off because I'm bored at home. I'm making more money than I ever have, and I'm busy—not doing the things that I need to do but doing the things I want to do. Once upon a time, I may have thought I wanted to make it big and vacation for the rest of my life. But I don't want to do nothing. I don't believe anyone truly does.

Franklin D. Roosevelt said, "Happiness is not in the mere possession of money; it lies in the joy of achievement, in the thrill of creative effort."

The most exciting part of my life is not the numbers in my bank account. It's helping others reach their visions.

If you believe that having lots of money is going to make you happy—that when you make it big, your work here is done—then you're going to be very unhappy once you do.

Money Magnifies

Robert Kiyosaki said, "Money only magnifies who you really are. If you are a happy person, more money will make you happier. If you are an unhappy person, more money will make you miserable."

You can see this in almost every instance of people winning the lottery or coming into massive amounts of wealth overnight. Here are just a few examples of this:

William "Bud" Post III won $16.2 million in the Pennsylvania Lottery in 1988. He received payouts of about $500,000 a year. By the end of the first year, he was already about $500,000 in debt. After years of mismanaging his money and making poor financial decisions, he filed for bankruptcy. When he passed away in 2006, he was $1 million in debt.[1]

David Lee Edwards won $27 million in the lottery in 2001. He lost all his money within five years. He and his wife were arrested multiple times in relation to drug charges. By the time he died in 2013, at the age of 58, he was living in a storage unit.[2]

Gerald Muswagon won $10 million in the lottery in 1998. He spent all of his winnings on partying. By 2005, he had run out of money and committed suicide.[3]

Evelyn Adams won the lottery twice, winning a total of $5.4 million between 1985 and 1986. By 2004, her winnings were completely gone, and she was living in a trailer park. She lost a large portion of the money gambling. [4]

Money itself was not necessarily the cause of their misfortunes. It's not money that's the problem. It's all the things that money magnifies in us. Do you have poor spending and saving habits? That won't change once you make your millions. Are you greedy or fearful that you will never have enough money? Having "enough" money won't change that. Are you struggling with expensive addictions? Money certainly isn't going to remove them from your life.

In one of my other books, *If I Won $25,000,000 in the Lottery*, I mentioned that whenever I think of the lottery, I am reminded of the 2005 movie "The Island." That analogy is worth revisiting here, too.

The movie starts out by making you believe the characters in the movie have survived a great holocaust. The characters believe they are trapped in a facility that is protecting them from the nuclear waste that has enveloped the earth. There, the characters are well taken care of. They have everything they need to comfortably survive—from the perfect temperature to the perfect food to the best exercises and even the best recreation. Their bodily fluids are constantly monitored to make sure that they are perfectly healthy.

Why would they ever want to leave?

They are told that as the earth clears away the nuclear waste, they will be the ones who are chosen to go into the world to live on the Island. It's everyone's dream. They believe it is a place of perfection—a place where everything will be even better. They will see trees and water and the sun—the real sun, and not just the fluorescent artificial lighting systems. The Island is where it will all begin again for them. Paradise!

The selection process is done by the lottery system. Everyone in the facility wishes for the day that their names are chosen. Whenever the lottery is drawn, all of the residents of the facility are called to the giant monitor where the names are drawn for the next set of lucky lottery winners. Then everyone else has to go back to their regular lives in the artificial environment where they waste their time wishing for the day it will be their turn to go to the island.

This movie has many social and political messages, but as the story goes on, you soon realize that the characters in the movie are just clones of the rich people living outside the compound. When they "win" the lottery, they are actually being selected to be killed so that their organs can be harvested in order to keep their copies alive.

There is no Island. There is only death.

So, why do I relate this movie to the lottery? Most people think that massive amounts of money will be the answer to all their problems. Paradise! But the truth is that most people who win the lottery become miserable. They lose their wealth almost as fast as they received it. Their entire lives are transformed—and not in a good way. It is not the perfect paradise they dreamed of. It is an unforgiving landscape that spits them back out again.

When you ask average Americans what they would do if they won the lottery, you can probably guess the average answers you're going to get: I would quit my job. I would move to an island. I would buy an island. I would buy a luxury car. I would party every night. I would live in a mansion. I'd sit on the beach drinking martinis for the rest of my life.

Those are just some of the answers you would get. Look at those responses. The fact is none of them truly have any substance. Those lives wouldn't have any substance.

What do you think of this question: Would you rather be rich, or would you rather be happy?

Okay, before you get too far into answering that question, I need to tell you that it's a stupid question! What the heck does being rich have to do with being happy, and what does being happy have to do with being rich? Nothing! They're not mutually exclusive at all. You can be poor and happy, you can be rich and happy; you can be poor and miserable, you can be rich and miserable. Therefore, money itself will never be the primary ingredient for happiness. But it's not the primary ingredient for misery, either. Your attitude and personal values will decide your happiness or misery levels—with or without money. Happiness and money are completely separate items, and one should not—and will not—cause the other to change.

Money Follows Natural Laws

Now, most fortunes do not come overnight. It's not likely that you will get your millions from playing the lottery or receiving an inheritance. There is mercy in that. If and when you join the millionaire club, it will more likely come as you slowly but surely grow into the mindset of a millionaire. It will be the natural result of cause and effect as you apply new principles and strategies in your life. The money will come to you as you earn it.

The people who are entrepreneurs, who are always driving themselves to be better and stronger—they have no choice but to get rich. Those people who are in it for the love of the game and the entrepreneurship, those are the people who will also be able to keep their wealth.

The people who just want to get rich just to fill their temporary needs of getting out of debt or splurging on buying themselves something fancy and nice are quickly going to run out of money and run out of purpose.

Everyone wants to be rich, but few think about the work and the mindset that are involved in maintaining that lifestyle.

Just remember that the principles that open financial doors for you are not necessarily the same doors that bring happiness and contentment. This is why I know that no matter how much money I make, I'm always going to be doing something. Because I have so much fun doing it! Helen Keller said, "True happiness is not attained through self-gratification, but through fidelity to a worthy purpose."

The doing, the learning, the creating, the teaching, the giving—every dollar I make feeds back into that mission and purpose. I will never be bored again.

That's the mind of a happy entrepreneur.

CHAPTER 5

Can Money Buy Happiness?

So, now let's talk about this quote that you've probably seen many times: Money can't buy happiness.

Do you believe this? I'm serious. Don't just give me an immediate answer. Think about it; pay attention to your feelings about it. Do you? Maybe you're not sure—or maybe you're not sure what the "right" answer is to the question—-especially after reading that last chapter—so, let's look a little closer at this idea of "happiness."

Paul Marturano, one of my students and colleagues, wrote a book called *33 Beliefs for a Happy Life*. Belief number fourteen is this:

We all want the same thing: to be loved and to be happy. It's what makes us human. It is the main reason for most of what we do. The secret to receiving love and happiness is to be the thing that you want. If you want love, be loving and it will come back to you. Happiness is a decision. We can decide to be happy. Happiness does not depend on achievement. It does not depend on events. Happiness is a state that is created by our reaction to events. No matter what happens in your life, it is your reaction to it that causes sadness, happiness, anger, joy, or whatever emotion you experience. We are in control of our reaction to events. That means we are in control of deciding if we are going to be happy or not.

Okay, so this gives us a sense of what creates happiness in our life. It hints at where it comes from, and there's nothing in there about being able to buy it off a shelf. But what *is* happiness? Can it be quantified? Can it be bought?

Wikipedia says: "The term happiness is used in the context of mental or emotional states, including positive or pleasant emotions ranging from contentment to intense joy. It is also used in the context of life satisfaction, subjective well-being, eudaimonia, flourishing, and well-being."

Eduamonia? What the heck does that mean? That's kind of a foreign word, isn't it? So, we're using words we don't know to try to understand other words we're trying to define. Hmm . . . The only rational conclusion I can come to is that, ultimately, we don't know what happiness is! So, how can we know if money can buy happiness if we don't even know how to quantify it?

Well, life gives clues, doesn't it? I mean, hopefully you have at least a general sense of whether or not you are happy. If someone walked up to you on the street and asked, "Are you happy today?" I hope you could give a pretty honest answer. We may not all agree on the definition of "happy," but I think we can all at least agree that (a) we know if we're happy or not, and (b) it isn't something on a shelf in the store. You can't go into a shop somewhere and say, "I would like two pounds of happiness, please."

So, let me ask you again: Can money buy happiness?

Let's see what my fellow entrepreneur Ely Delaney has to say about it:

"Money Can't Buy Happiness" . . . is a lie. We've all heard this phrase before. Usually from well-intended family or friends. The problem is that it's just not true.

Will having money make you happy, most likely not. It in itself is just a tool. However, depending on how you use that money, you can become one of the happiest people on Earth.

As I write this, I'm typing this as my first work on a brand-new MacBook Pro. But what is special about this is that this was a gift from a client.

Call it a birthday present (my birthday is this weekend).

Call it a Christmas present (next month).

Call it an end-of-year bonus (also next month).

Call it a gift of appreciation for helping them grow their business (which we've all worked hard for).

Call it all of those together (which is totally appropriate for such an awesome gift).

. . . This gift means more to me than I think they would have thought (which it's freaking awesome, by the way!). See, they didn't need to do it. I didn't ask for it. We were talking, and I mentioned that my six-plus-year-old laptop was finally giving me trouble that was beyond just cleaning it up and I needed to get a new one soon (Black Friday coming up and all).

It just showed up yesterday with a nice note thanking me for helping put their company on the map.

I was just shocked.

But I want you to stop and pay attention here. The laptop is amazing, but that's NOT what made me happy. It was the feeling that I got because of receiving such a great gift. It was the feeling that I know I am appreciated. It was the feeling that I make enough of a difference for them that they took the time. It was that someone wanted to do that for me.

Those things are why I was so happy.

I actually cried in my car with happiness that someone took the time to appreciate me that much and I KNEW right there that I made a difference.

Was it about the laptop itself?

No. It's just a thing. (Don't get me wrong, it's a freaking MacBook Pro. I'm super excited about this thing.) The feeling I had at that moment was pure happiness that I've rarely felt before.

When someone does something nice for you, be in appreciation of it, and it's a great reason to be happy.

BUT that's not even the end of it . . .

Money CAN buy happiness.

When I called them to thank them for the amazing gift, I could hear THEIR happiness over the phone—the happiness they got from being able to make my day better. I know that my call made their day. I just know it. I know that feeling. I've had that feeling before . . .

So if you ask me if I believe money can buy happiness—yes, I do 100 percent. Just not in the way that most people think it does. [1]

Those are some interesting thoughts on happiness, don't you agree? (And by the way, Ely was correct. The person on the phone was extremely happy. I know because that person was me.)

Now I want to share another story with you. This one is a bit closer to home. I'm in a bunch of entrepreneur groups on Facebook, and during the COVID pandemic, someone made a post that read something like this: How can someone who has nothing become an entrepreneur when they have nothing to give?

I immediately responded back and said:

Step 1: Stop believing you have nothing to give.

Step 2: Contact me as soon as you do step one.

Five minutes later, he sent me a private message, in which he said, "I don't know what I have to offer."

So, I asked him what he liked to do. He said he liked to help people—he wanted to be a philanthropist.

Okay, time out for a second. Let me speak to this whole "philanthropist" thing. I don't think anyone actually wants to be a philanthropist—they want to be nice to people. And that's cool. But true philanthropy is not what most people think it is. You don't have to wait until you're a millionaire to help people or to start changing people's lives. If you tell me you want to be a philanthropist, I don't buy it. It's a smoke screen for something else. What you're really telling me is that you want to help people *someday*—but for now, you don't feel like you have enough resources to go around and make a difference. But that mindset has nothing to do with how much money is in your wallet.

So anyway—this guy told me he wanted to be a philanthropist. I asked him what he wanted to do, and he said he really wanted to help children and he could teach them to play basketball, and he was going on and on in that vein of what *he* believes is philanthropy, and I was about to write him off because I was getting really annoyed with all of that. Finally, I butted it and said, "Listen, what do you have to offer?" And he boiled it down to this: I want to help kids get out of bad neighborhoods and make something of their lives.

"How do you want to do that?" I asked.

"I don't know," he said. "I don't have anything. As a matter of fact, all I have to my name is $87. My car is broken, and that's going to be an $800 repair. I can't drive anywhere and haven't been able to in a while. What *can* I do?"

I said, "Here's what you can do: go buy two gift cards—$25 each—and give them away."

"I only have $87 to my name! What exactly am I supposed to do here?!"

I just repeated myself. "Go buy two gift cards—$25 each—and give them away."

"Come on," he said. "There's gotta be something else I can do."

"Dude," I said, "are you coachable? Because I'm not going to be able to help you if you're not coachable."

"Yes, I'm coachable."

"Okay, then go buy those gift cards."

"And then what?"

And, well, I'll let him tell you about it in his own words:

I woke up to a cold November rainy day and gave thanks to God, as per my usual morning ritual because it has a tendency to get my day started off on the right side of productive. I checked my Facebook and noticed a group of entrepreneurs was offering me advice on how to overcome financial adversity—all of which were in response to my post. I was set on taking everybody's advice, but the first comment captured my attention. It was posted by a gent that I knew nothing of. His comment read, "Step 1 is to stop thinking you have nothing. When you have that step completed, contact me for step 2."

I was very intrigued as to what advice this gent by the name of Larry Steinhouse could have for me in terms of knowledge and wisdom, so I took him up on his offer and reached out to Mr. Steinhouse, with the utmost respect for him being willing to take time out of his day to guide me in the right direction. I reached out to Larry via [Facebook] Messenger, and we chatted for longer than I expected.

I was pleased to know that Larry was a man of faith like myself, and I felt like he would be like a big brother to me. As our chat helped us build rapport with one another, Mr. Steinhouse earned my respect with his choice of words and his confidence in leading me. Larry asked, "What is it that you would like to do?" I said I would like to be a philanthropist and a motivational speaker. It was at that point that Larry asked if I was coachable. I responded with complete confidence that I didn't know existed with me. Larry said, "I want you to go buy two $25 gift cards and randomly give them away to two individuals. The only stipulation is that you have to ask God's direction on who to give them to." Larry made it seem like this was an easy feat to accomplish, but little did he know my financial situation was a complete wreck.

I had a total of $87 to my name, and he wanted me to go give over half of it away. The thought within myself was that I am in no position whatsoever to just go give away over half of my money. I had mentioned my financial situation to Larry, and he completely disregarded it and redirected me back to the mission. I'm familiar with the term "Act of Good Faith," and that's all that I could feel within my mind and body as he urged me to complete the mission. I told Larry, "I can't wait to see what the moral to this story is," and he replied, "Maybe there's no moral to the story." That was somewhat discouraging at the moment, but the light was on and I was going to complete this mission, no matter what, because I could feel a goodness that was unexplainable. I literally felt compelled to abide by Mr. Steinhouse's direction as if he were a prophet.

My car is broken down, so I had to walk to the Walmart in the rain. As I walked, an evil presence slithered its way into my thought process. I found myself devising a plan that would shortchange the mission, allowing me to keep the majority of my cash by purchasing the $25 cards, taking pics [to send to Larry], and then pulling all but $6 dollars out, leaving whomever I gave the cards to $3 instead of $25 per card.

The good within assured me that I would only be shortchanging myself, so I decided to go with good over evil, which is a lot easier for me to do these days. I was all in with this act of good faith, and nothing was going to deter me from accomplishing my goal to follow through 100 percent.

I made it to the Walmart, purchased the gift cards, and wandered aimlessly through the aisles of Walmart, waiting for a voice or calling to point someone out for me to bless during these hard times that this pandemic has created for people all throughout the world.

I kept trying to zero in on single parents with children, but every time, I felt an undeniable intuition say "no" or "keep moving." I made my way from the toy section to the produce aisles, and that's when I saw a Hispanic guy that was shopping all by his lonesome. He was bagging a decent amount of veggies in each bag, insinuating he had a family. I felt an enlightening feeling come over me. He was the first person I was meant to bless for the day, so I acted as if I were going to look at avocados and did my best to perceive and make sure that I was being led by a prophetic message and not counsel of the wicked. There was an overwhelming presence assuring me that he was worthy of this good deed.

The closer I got, the more evident it became that I should bless the guy with the gift card. So I stopped him and said, "Hi, I'm a firm believer in God, and I am feeling an overwhelming feeling to help you today."

He seemed startled. I obviously caught him off guard because he was saying, "Oh, okay, thank you," but he was still walking without allowing me to hand him the gift card. So I reiterated, in a more authoritative tone, that this card was meant for him. I said, "I would like to pay for some of your food." He stopped and kind of cocked his head to the side in a "Are you sure this is meant for me?" kind of way. As he took the card, he seemed to be very skeptical and genuinely pleased at the same time. He thanked me with a simple smile that shown through his COVID-19 mask. It was easily the best feeling I had felt since the birth of my son. My mission was only halfway completed, and I had a wonderful feeling within myself.

As I was walking away, I noticed he was scratching the card and getting prepared to check the balance on the card with his phone. I asked if I could take a picture with him and be on my way. He said sure. I took the picture and sent it to Larry and assured him I would check in with him after the mission was complete. His response was, "Awesome!"

I wandered around the store for thirty minutes, and I even got to the point where I thought that maybe I should go back to the shopping center across the street. I was asking God to guide me, and I thought to myself, What is all this for? And it was like the entire store got quiet. Just then, a little old lady's voice said, "Thank you." I had to find that lady, and I found her about three aisles away. I passed her by, waiting to see if she was meant to be helped. I started my thought process all over again, and sure enough, I felt called to add a little holiday cheer to her life. It was something equivalent to a celebratory or harmonious feeling. There was no doubt whatsoever. She was all smiles and happiness even before I mentioned helping her out. The oddity was that she was completely oblivious to the fact that I had likened her to that of God's angel. Her positivity was the best to be around, her spirit was that of a good one.

I handed her the gift card without hesitation. I let her know that I was a firm believer in God and that I would like to pay for a portion of her items by giving her a gift card. She cracked the biggest smile ever, and I felt a goodness all throughout my mind, body, and soul.

I was wearing my Tim Duncan Spurs jersey, and she told me before I left, "You are totally wearing the right jersey for this occasion because this is exactly the acts of good faith Tim Duncan does in the community." We hugged—against social distancing standards—we took a pic, made a short video, and went on our ways.

On my way out of the Walmart, the first guy stopped me so that his family could say thank you via Facetime. We took one more pic together and I was on my way.

At this point, I was so very thankful for Larry Steinhouse putting me up to this that there's nothing I wouldn't do for this man because he is a man of faith like me and therefore my brother in Christ as well as in life. I sent the last pic to Larry, along with a text that said, "Mission Accomplished." I said the lady and the gentleman were very happy, as was I. His response was, "And you were the happiest of all," which was true.

Larry went on to say, "Today you were everything you said you wanted to be, and it only cost you $50."[5]

Okay, I want you to think about this. Take a few steps back. How much money was spent? Fifty dollars. How many people were made happy? Four! Who was the happiest? You might guess it was the guy who handed out the gift cards—I told him it was—but I'm going to go out on a limb and say it was me. I was overjoyed!

But wait . . . there's more!

Here's what happened next. I told him, "Hold on, I have an additional assignment for you. I want you to write down and journal what just happened." He immediately went home and followed my instructions to a T. He sent me what he wrote down (which was handwritten, by the way, because he didn't have a computer), and I was like *Holy Crap! This guy can WRITE!*

I asked him if I could pay him $500 for the rights to his story. He was ecstatic. "Yes!" he said. "That's great! That's wonderful!"

I immediately sent him the money for his story, and now here it is in my book, told exactly the way he wrote it down.

Shortly after that, he mailed me a gift. I opened it up and found his personal copy of Max Lucado's book *The Gift for All People: Thoughts on God's Great Grace*. Included with the gift was this note:

It is with great appreciation and gratitude that I pray this gift that I have chosen for you provides light and a sense that only a good brother like yourself can perceive. My only hope is that I could have sent you something of more worth from a worldly perspective. You've now sparked a fire within me that will only continue to grow and burn with more passion and determination than you could ever know. For that, I thank you. I pray my Lord Jesus will ask God to bless you with good health and more years of good prosperity—a good decision, as per request. I also pray that God blesses you with an abundance of knowledge, wisdom, and understanding so that you may be without doubt in your decision-making process. Amen, my brother. Much Love, Justin.

I immediately reached out to thank him for the gift. He again told me that he just wished he could have sent me something new. I told him, "No way!" There was nothing new he could have sent me that was better than that book. It was something he had cherished—and it's something I cherish now, too, and that has become part of my school.

So, let's go back to our question. Can money buy happiness?

Well, by now, I hope you know the answer to that question. And if you're not sure yet, I want you to go out yourself and buy two $100 gift cards. Do not just randomly give them away. Let God guide you to the people you're supposed to give them to. I promise you that you will hear your heart tell you who the right people are. That will be the beginning of a domino effect of happiness that will come full circle, all the way back to you.

Can money buy happiness? Well, I think the better question—the only question that mattered in the first place—is this: Who are YOU going to buy happiness for?

CHAPTER 6

Coaches and Mentors

One of my mentors is my current business partner, Phil Falcone. Before he and I went into business together to create our investor's school (InvestorSchooling.com), he was just the real estate mogul I hung around with for a long time. We met post 2008. I was still doing some real estate deals, but it wasn't my main source of income. I had a J-O-B at the time. I was making over six figures, so I felt pretty secure. It was a job I hated, mind you. But it paid my bills, and I liked the promise of another paycheck.

The real estate was still on my radar, though. I mean, I'd been doing real estate deals since I was 18. I was never going to drop it completely. And Phil was a great mentor. He owned a business called Addicted to Real Estate, and he'd written multiple books. I really enjoyed spending time with him and learning from him. But every time I would go in and meet with him at his office, he would look me square in the face and say, "Larry, quit your job. You will make more money."

It bugged me. I would say, "Are you out of your mind? I'm making six figures!" He'd just shake his head and tell me to quit my job. We had this conversation almost every . . . single . . . time I went into his office. Finally, I'd walk in and see him open his mouth, and before he could say anything, I would put my hands up and say, "I know, I know! 'Quit your job, you'll make more money.' I've heard you say it a million times. Shut up already!"

"Well," he'd say. "If you quit your job, you would."

This went on for a long time, until—guess what happened—I lost that six-figure job. And you know what? Six months later, I was making just as much money as I'd been making at my J-O-B and I was doing something I really loved.

The next year, I made more than my previous salary. The following year, I made four times my previous salary. Now I'm making even more than that. And it's consistent. Before, I was counting on that paycheck from week to week and I made sacrifices to make sure I'd have it. But now, the money is like a game to me. If I had the same amount of money coming to me every Friday, I think I'd die of boredom.

This just goes to show that if you decide you're going to do something—and you're working with a qualified mentor who has the map to where you want to go, and you get your mindset in the right place—you can really make a difference. You can make things happen.

How many mentors have you had? How many do you currently have? I won't take "zero" for an answer. Having a mentor or a coach is an absolute must.

Coaches Don't Coddle

Often, people come to me for real estate coaching and say, "Can you help me find a property?" So, I go down the list of steps: I tell them to send out this letter, go to these areas, and go talk to those people. And then, sometimes, they go cross-eyed and say, "No—I mean, can you find a property for me?" Then things get really quiet.

I just look at them and say, "Let me get this straight. You think that if I find a good deal that I am going to hand it over to you? No. I am going to teach you how to find them yourself. But don't worry—when you find them and don't know how to fund them, I want you to come to me and I will help you get the money and maybe even partner with you on the deal."

A coach is not someone who is going to start loading up your plate with fish. They are going to give you a fishing pole and help you learn to cast. No one can do it for you.

My wife always accuses me of being mean to my students. But I'm not being mean. I'm being blunt. I don't have time to be anything else. Afterall, I'm getting paid to coach my students. They don't want to have to wade through PC crap to get what they paid for. So, I tell them like it is. As a consultant, I like to think of it like this: I am an insultant so you can become a resultant. (This is a quote from David Corbin, another one of my mentors.)

This works.

When I repeat back to you what you just said and—don't take offense here—it sounds stupid to you, I have done you a great service, because now you know how stupid it was. I do this often. If you decide to coach with me, you should expect to squirm a little. Don't get me wrong, I'm no drill sergeant. I'm not going to step up and yell in your face or make you do push-ups if you don't do things my way.

But I am going to pull you out of your comfort zone, and I'm going to challenge your thinking on things. How else will you evolve into the next version of yourself?

One of the coaches I'm working with really makes me squirm. There are times I am so uncomfortable that it almost drives me crazy. For instance, I am supposed to be gluten free. He keeps me accountable to that because he understands that my physical health is an important part of my mental health, which is an important part of my success mentality and to my financial fitness. Well, the other day I sent him a picture of a cake I was eating. I sent it to him as a friend. But he didn't break character for a second. As my coach, he yelled at me. Because that's how cool this guy is. That's how much he wants to make sure my life is like his life (by the way, he's a billionaire).

A great mentor will always tell you what you need to hear, not what you want to hear. Remember when my mentor kept telling me to quit my job? It pissed me off. But I really needed to hear that—even if I didn't want to hear it at all. Who else do you think was giving me that advice? Nobody. But he knew because he was on the other side of those life choices. He could see very clearly what others—including myself—could not see at all.

Coaches are Aliens

I will never *not* have coaches and mentors around me. Right now, I am actively working with four different coaches. As I already mentioned, one of those coaches is a billionaire—his name is Brian. How easy do you think it would be to be jealous of that guy? Well, I'm not. Instead, I see him as someone who can teach me how to be in his shoes one day.

Lucky for me, billionaires usually like to talk to people. They're actually pretty down to earth. My billionaire-coach and I talk every Tuesday night. We have a standing appointment. And let me tell you, we have some of the oddest conversations. Well, odd for me, anyway. Talking to a billionaire is a different experience. I have to really stretch myself to get onto his level.

I don't mean this as an insult to anyone reading this book, but the only thing I can compare it to is my distaste for banal conversation about TV shows or social media drama. I just can't get into those kinds of conversations. They bore me. I don't have time for TV or celebrities' relationship problems. I'm too busy going out into the world and making deals! I'm building my business and I'm growing.

But it's as if I'm playing Hopscotch compared to Brian. Right now, I have to replace a water heater in one of the properties I'm rehabbing. I am so irritated by this. But this guy has to build a wing onto a hospital. Wow, that's a really different set of problems, isn't it?

A few weeks ago, he called me up at our regular time and said, "I'm sorry—I have to coach you from my car today because I have to go to the shopping center."

"Oh, are you going shopping?" I asked.

"No, no, no—I own a 300,000-square-foot shopping center, and one of my tenants has to sign a new lease. They didn't like some of the terms, and my guys couldn't work it out. I am going to go take care of it."

"Oh! Who is the tenant?" I asked.

"It's Barnes & Noble."

See what I mean? He's on a completely different level.

I definitely have to step outside of my comfort zone when I'm talking to this coach. But I'm okay with that, because he is where I want to be. I want to go into his arena and talk to people like him. Even if it's uncomfortable. In fact, especially if it's uncomfortable. In order to participate in the conversation there, I have to stretch myself. If I'm stretching, I'm growing.

Seek Counsel—Not Opinion

Here's something to keep in mind—a quote from another great mind, Greg Reid: "Successful people seek counsel, where failures listen to opinion."

How many people do you know who have started a project or talked about some of their ambitions and their entire family told them not to do it because it wouldn't work? MLMs are a perfect example of this. Whether you like them or not, it doesn't matter—the point is that if you are excited about it, why is your family beating you down? "Oh, that's a stupid idea. I tried that years ago. It's just a scheme. They never work." Really? Because I know many people in the MLM industry who are in early retirement from the money they've made on those opportunities.

Or how about real estate investment? "Why would anyone want to buy real estate now? Prices are too high. The next bubble is coming."

These are nothing but opinions. And they are driven by fear or inexperience or blindness. Counsel is what will get you to the next level. Counsel comes with blueprints and strategies from those on the other side.

I'm telling you, don't listen to broke people.

When I told my mother I was being coached by a billionaire, she laughed at me. She didn't laugh at me because she was laughing *at* me. She laughed because she was so uncomfortable by the idea of it;

it was so surreal to her that laughing was the only reaction she could come up with. Why would she do that? It's because she didn't get it.

Someone's opinion of you—or what you should and should not be doing—should never become your reality. This can be hard when it's someone who is close to you and who is supposed to want what's best for you. My own father used to be my worst enemy when it came to my success. He's now deceased, and sometimes I still have to do some work to get him out of my head.

When I wrote my first book, I told my dad I was writing a book about money. He laughed. He sarcastically said, "Just what the world needs—another book about money." It wasn't, "Wow, Larry, that's awesome that you wrote a book!" It wasn't, "That's amazing! I know you have been helping me with money for years, so I bet you will help a lot of people with your book."

No. Instead, it was a biting criticism. He basically told me I was wasting my time. And let me tell you, I heard a lot of unspoken words in those few words he said.

I didn't like that I didn't have my own father's support. There might be people in your life like this, too. But you have to remember that the opinion of those people is not nearly as important as the opinion you have of yourself. And that should never be dictated by another human being. They don't have the right to write that script for you. Don't give them that power.

So, what's your opinion of yourself? Do you believe you have what it takes to master the strategies in this book? Do you believe you have the power to do everything you set out to do? I know some people who think so highly of themselves that they have to catch up to themselves. By the way, I am one of them. Somebody called me arrogant once, and I found it a compliment. (That may or may not be a joke . . .)

What (or Who) Will You Sacrifice for Your Dreams?

If you're going to get the most out of your mentor and coaching experiences, you need to be willing to step outside of your comfort zone—it's going to cost you. What are you willing to give up in order to reach your next level? Some of your time? Some of your TV shows? Some of your limiting beliefs about money?

How about some of your friends?

Does that one hit a soft spot for you? That can be hard to accept—or to even understand. But listen, if you have friends who are pulling you down, are they actually good friends? Is there someone in your life who, every time you talk about an opportunity or an investment deal, tells you not to do it? Or that you're just dreaming? How about this one: "That's a get-rich-quick scheme."

I guarantee you've heard some of these exact statements before. If you're reading this book, that means you're working to break the mold. You're willing to step outside of your comfort zone. And there are going to be people in your life who don't like that. They want you to stay exactly where you are—because that is where *they* are comfortable. Do you understand what I'm saying? They're not ready to stretch with you. It doesn't feel good.

So, sometimes you have to give them up. Life is a team sport! The question is: Who is on your team? You should always choose your team with intention. You are the product of the five people you hang around the most. That's true today, and it will be true a year from now. If you want to be further ahead in your goals a year from now, you might have to change up those five people a little bit.

Who are you hanging around?

If you're taking an inventory of those five people and you're seeing some "weak links," I hope you'll choose to take a step up. When you do, you might have to leave some people behind. Not because you are abandoning your friends but because they aren't going to step up with you. This is an important distinction for you to understand. You aren't leaving anyone. It's just that some people will refuse to follow where you're going.

But don't let that deter you from going there. If you step up and they don't, keep facing forward. Let it happen. Don't look back, or they're going to pounce. Trust me. They're waiting for their chance to drag you back down. This doesn't mean they're trying to hurt you or that they want you to fail. And it doesn't mean you can't call your friends or family members and ask how they are doing. I'm not suggesting that you completely cut your loved ones out of your life. But I am saying you have to be careful not to let them drag you back into *their* comfort zones.

If you have ever left a toxic relationship with someone who held you back in your life, you know exactly what I am talking about. I was married to someone who held me back so bad I could barely breathe. It was a suffocating experience. The second I escaped from that marriage, things changed. I am not advocating divorce—don't misunderstand me—but if you've been there, you get it. Sometimes you have to cut out the cancer.

The safest and most effective way to do this is to surround yourself with the mentors and the coaches who will be there to remind you of what's possible. They've been where you are now, and they've made it to the next level. They have muscle memory for the way there. They don't just see your goals as possibilities, they see them as turn-key opportunities. You just need the right key—and they can give it to you.

Pay Your Coaches and Mentors

Having a coach or a mentor is going to cost you in other ways, too. It's going to cost you some money—as it should! This is going to sound crazy, but you *want* to pay your coaches. Trust me on this one.

A few years ago, before we opened Investor Schooling, someone called me up and said, "Hey, can you teach me a little bit about real estate?"

I said, "Alright, sure!"

So, I met him just around the corner at our local Dunkin Donuts. I gave him some ideas and advised him on a couple things he should do to get started. A week later, I called to follow up with him.

He had done nothing.

"Why haven't you done anything?" I asked.

"Oh, I just wasn't ready," he said.

He wasted my time for a cup of coffee.

A couple weeks later, someone else called me up and said, "Hey, can you tell me a little bit about stock options?"

I said, "Sure!"

We met up for lunch, and it felt good to open my brain to someone. It stroked my ego a little bit, and I sincerely felt like I was helping someone. I gave him insider secrets that only come from experience—years and years of successes and failures. I was truly giving him a jump on the learning curve. I gave my friend some tips and advised him on how to get started. A week later, I called him up and asked, "So, what'd you do?"

Nothing.

Two for two.

I was getting a little frustrated. Not only had these guys wasted my time, but they failed to see the value of what I'd given them.

They were still just going back to the daily grind, doing everything the way they'd always done it, heading for the same destination as before. They were still on a nowhere road leading to a nowhere place.

A couple weeks later, I got a call from someone else. "Hey, can you tell me a little bit about real estate?"

I said, "Yes—that will be $3,500 for coaching."

He was happy to pay it. So, we met up for lunch and I give him the same tips and advice I gave to friend number-one. A week later, I followed up with him to see how it was going.

He had started applying everything I taught him.

From that experience, I learned that you have to pay in order to pay attention.

It's that simple, and it's the truth. If you start paying a coach and you have that meeting at 2:30 PM on Tuesday, guess where you are going to be at 2:30 PM on Tuesday? You are going to have your butt in that seat, ready to talk to your coach because you paid for it. When you pay, you pay attention.

Don't Let Greed Keep You from Growth

Many people in this world will never benefit from having a coach or a mentor because they can't get over their own greed. They covet the money they have, and they covet the money they don't have. These are the people who feel entitled to the riches and success that belong to those who could have been their mentors. They believe it's unfair for successful people to have "all that money." They think successful people should be bled with taxes so that the wealth can be more evenly distributed among everyone else. "That's the only way to be fair!" they say. "They need to give their money to the poor!"

But what they're really saying is, "Give some of that money to *me*."

It is often the people without money who covet other people's money the most. They are greedy for the things they don't even have. And that's why they can't learn how to get them. If you busy yourself with coveting the money of others—or even the money you already have—you will never have the time or the ability to devote any energy to trying to be successful yourself or to evolve beyond where you are right now.

Instead of being jealous, it's important to recognize that most of the people who have wealth have earned it. Yes, there are some people who have inherited their lifestyles—but that money first came from someone else who earned it. They followed ancient, proven formulas that unlock that kind of wealth. Those formulas often include doing the things that bring people up in society. They do it by following many of the strategies outlined in this book.

How else have they done it? Well, it's your job to find out.

Go ask them.

Go hire them.

Go follow them.

And don't forget to give back!

CHAPTER 7

The Truth About Credit Scores

One thing my mentors have always shown me is that your past—whatever it is—does not have to define your future. There is always a way up and out of whatever financial situation you're in right now. If you're going to believe that, you have to start by forgetting everything you've ever been told about your credit score. It does not own you. It does not rule your life. Believe that, and it will no longer have the power to *ruin* your life.

In 2008, I was riding the peak of the real estate wave . . . until I lost everything.

I'd made some clear mistakes in some properties I bought, and I decided the best way to solve my problem was bankruptcy. It was a calculated business decision. At the time, I owed $3 million on $3.9 million of real estate. The value of that real estate dropped to $2.5

million overnight. By the time I went through bankruptcy, it had fallen to $1.2 million, and by the time the bank sold it off, it was sold for $750,000.

Bankruptcy was the best business decision I ever made. It gave me the opportunity to wipe out all of those mistakes and start over again with a clean slate.

Today, my credit score is always hovering in the 680 to 750 range. I have multiple lines of credit in good standing—and I'm consistently adding more lines of credit all the time. My bankruptcy has no control over my life. I am free. Free to do and to build and to grow as much as I want to.

Regardless of where you're starting from today, I'm going to show you how you can get your personal credit score in the 680 to 750 range—and keep it there. Once you master that, you won't believe the doors that will open for you.

Credit Score Reality

First, you need to have a better understanding of credit score reality. Let's start by looking at two credit scores side by side:

720 850

What are the differences between these two credit scores? Would you say it's buying power? Would you say it's your lendability? The answer is nothing. If you have an 850 credit score and you go in to get a mortgage, you're going to get the same interest rate you'd get with a 720 credit score. If you go to get a car loan and you have an 850 credit score, your interest rate is going to be the same as if you came in with a 720 credit score. *There is no difference*. This is one of the most important concepts I need you to understand: No one cares if you have an 850 credit score. It's not going to open any more doors for you than a 720 will. In fact, I would argue that if you have an 850 credit score, you're wasting it. You can actually leverage the other 130 points in order to strengthen your lendability.

In order to understand this, you need to know how your score is calculated in the first place.

How Your Credit Score is Calculated

Your credit can range anywhere from 300 to 850. You get that first 300 just by being born. It's kind of like the SATs you took in high school, where you got a certain number of points just by writing your name on the top of the test. You get those first 300 points of your credit score just by having a name and social security number, which means they basically add zero value to your score. The actual credit score range is zero to 550 because those are the points you can actually manipulate and control. Once you understand that, the rest of the math I'm going to show you will make sense.

Here's the breakdown of where the rest of your points come from (the percentages are based on that 550):

35%	192.5 points	Making your payments on time
30%	165 points	How much of your available credit is being used
15%	82.5 points	The average age of your credit
10%	55 points	The types of credit you have
10%	55 points	Inquiries on your credit

550 points
+300 FREE
850 POINTS

Making Your Payments on Time

The number one most important thing affecting your credit score is whether or not you're making your payments on time. This accounts for 35 percent of your score—a whopping 192.5 points (rounded up to 193). The ratio here is almost one to one—if you miss one payment, expect it to cost you 10 percent of these points (19 points). If you have two late payments, expect a 20 percent hit. By the time you get to four, five, and six late payments, though, the percentage no longer matters; no one is going to give you a mortgage anyway.

Plain and simple, my advice is to never make a late payment. Borrow money from your credit cards to pay the car loan if you have to—but *do not* make a late payment. I'm going to be brutally honest with you—if you don't make your payments on time, everything else I'm going to teach you is going to be worthless to you. But if you are committed to making your payments on time, you're doing pretty good right out of the gate.

A late payment is anything thirty days or more past the due date. Not everyone reports on that thirty-first day, but there's no telling who uses what standard, so don't chance it. Just pay before you hit that thirty-day mark. If you end up making a late payment, and it's your first time making one on that account, call the lender and let him know you just forgot and ask him to waive the late fee and agree not to report the late payment. If it's your first time missing the payment, he may help you out. But don't rely on that, and you certainly shouldn't expect him to repeat the favor if he does.

Verizon once made a mistake on their end and failed to record my payment. I got a letter from a credit collector a few weeks later demanding the payment, which was the first I knew of the situation. I called and got it cleared up but check this out—that one late payment on my credit dropped my score by forty points. Forty points! For one $80 payment! I fought it, and the whole thing was taken care of—they sent me an apology letter, my credit score was restored, yadda yadda—but I just could not get over how huge of a hit that set me back in the meantime. That was the first time my credit score went below 700 in years. So yes—you better believe that those late payments are going to be the factor that hurts you the most.

How Much of Your Available Credit is Being Used

The second biggest chunk of your score comes from how much of your available credit is being used. This makes up 30 percent, or 165 points, of your credit score. This number is calculated based on how far you've maxed out your lines of credit—specifically your credit cards. If you keep the amount of money borrowed under 10 percent of what you can borrow, you're going to keep all 165 points. The higher that percentage goes up, the bigger the hit to your credit score.

For the sake of easy math, let's say you have $100,000 available to you in credit cards. As long as you borrow no more than $10,000 (10 percent) against those lines of credit, your credit score isn't going to take any hits. If you borrow $50,000 (50 percent), those 165 points are going to be cut in half—you'll get an 82.5-point ding. If you borrow close to the full amount—100 percent—you'll lose all 165 points.

So, let's say I have $450,000 of credit cards in my hand right now. That means I can borrow up to $45,000 before it has any effect on my credit score. Not bad.

It sounds pretty straight forward, but this factor is one of the least understood. You see, most people think that the only way to manipulate this number is to pay down your credit cards. But there's also another way. Your second option is to raise the amount of credit available to you. Let's say you owe $15,000 on your $100,000 line of credit, which comes to 15 percent. You can pay that down to $10,000 to restore all of those 165 points, or you can get another credit card for $50,000. That would bring your total available credit to $150,000, effectively bringing your borrowed $15,000 into that magical 10 percent range.

This is the number one trick I use. If you leverage this strategy effectively, you can raise your credit score as much as 50 points in a week. I've done it. My students have done it. This is a proven strategy for raising your credit score almost instantly.

By now, you're probably asking how the heck it's possible to raise the amount of credit available to you high enough to make that big of a difference. Well, if you can't get your line of credit up that high on your own, you can piggyback off someone else's lines of credit. You can find close friends or relatives who have a high-limit credit card and have them add you to their lines of credit—not as an authorized user, of course, but your name (i.e., your credit score) will be associated with those accounts and you'll see the effects of that right away.

Let's say, for example, you needed to add $30,000 to your available credit. You might call your mom and say, "Can you do me a favor and add me to your credit card? Don't worry, I'm not going to use it. Shred my card when it comes in the mail—I want you to destroy it. I don't ever want to see it. I just need the help with my credit score." Then, her $30,000 line of credit gets added to *your* available credit. Once that number goes up, the percentage you've borrowed goes down.

Some of my students have done this and gotten anywhere from fifty to seventy points added to their credit score almost instantly. They qualified for mortgage loans they didn't qualify for just days before.

I've proved that this works, and I will keep proving it. When you understand the rules of credit, you can manipulate your credit score like you never have before.

Age of Credit

The next factor affecting your credit score is the average age of your credit, which accounts for 15 percent, or 82.5 points (rounded up to 83 points) of your score. The older your credit, the higher your score. Ten years is the golden number. Once you hit the ten-year mark, you will have all 83 points. This is why older people naturally have higher credit scores. They've just had their lines of credit open longer.

When I first started applying for credit cards again in 2009, I was getting declined like crazy. Finally, I was approved for a $500 Capital One card. That's all I was able to get. Then, in 2010, that line of credit went up to $750 simply because it was a year older. Then, all of a sudden, I was approved for another credit card for $1,500, and then another card for $2,000. However, it's important to keep in mind that this factor looks at the average age of your credit. My first credit card after the bankruptcy dates back over ten years ago, but I've secured the bulk of my credit lines over the last four years. So, the average age of my credit probably sits at about five years. That takes about 42 points off my credit score, but that number will go down year after year.

It's important to note that it's better to have more lines of credit than it is to have a higher age of credit. If you have three credit cards that are ten years old and you apply for three new cards today and get all of them approved, your average age is now five years, but the sacrifice builds your credit score on the other side. It feeds back into that 30 percent coming from the amount of credit you have and are using, which is the more important number.

The Types of Credit You Have

This next one, the types of credit you have, accounts for 10 percent, or 55 points, of your score, but it's a little vague. What's the exact ratio of the kinds of credit you should have? Well, I haven't been able to find anyone who can completely answer that question for me, but the experts I've talked to all say the same thing: Just have multiple types of credit and you will get the full 55 points. There is no concrete breakdown. Just understand that it's important to have multiple types of credit. If you have just credit cards, you're probably going to get half of the points that come from this factor. If you have a car loan, some personal loans or mortgages, and a credit card or two, you are likely going to get the full 55 points.

Credit Inquiries

Credit inquiries account for 10 percent, or 55 points, of your credit score. I can almost guarantee you know a lot less about this particular factor than you think you do. Let's say you're trying to get a loan so you can buy a house. How bad is it going to hurt your credit if you have ten inquiries? Honestly, that kind of depends. On the one hand, having ten inquiries is going to hit that pool of 55 points pretty hard. On the other hand, you may be applying for credit and getting it, which would lower the overall percentage of money you're borrowing against the credit available to you and raise your credit score on the other side. Still, it's a crapshoot, and I agree with the mortgage lenders—average people shouldn't be getting inquiries when they're trying to get a loan. I've had clients lose the ability to buy a house because they applied for credit at the same time they were trying to buy a house. The rule of thumb here is to avoid inquiries for at least six months before you are considering a mortgage and until the day after you close.

So, if we agree that ten inquiries is going to make a dent in your credit score, what about twenty? Or thirty? What about forty-six? Do you think that person is likely to get approved for a mortgage? Hmmm . . . Let's talk about that. We'd all agree that someone with a 720 credit score is absolutely going to get approved for a loan, right? Well, is it possible to have 720 and 46 inquiries on your credit?

Absolutely. I know because I have just described myself.

Here's how that's possible: Inquiries only account for 55 points of your credit score—period. Once you hit ten inquiries, you've wiped out the entire 55 points. It doesn't matter how many inquiries you have after that. I am positive this is true. I experimented with my own credit score to prove it. A year ago, my credit score was about 805. I wanted to see how many inquiries it would take to move my score below 720. I racked up inquiry after inquiry. I watched the number go down—until it hit 750. It didn't budge after that, despite the fact that I slammed it with thirty-six more inquiries. I do this kind of experimenting all the time because I'm never going to give you advice I haven't followed. I sacrifice my own credit score so that I can teach you first-hand knowledge about the reality of what works and what doesn't.

Bringing it All Together

Now that you know the breakdown of what's creating your actual credit score and how to manipulate those factors to your benefit, let's bring it all together and look at how this all works out for you when you're trying to get a loan:

You start with the free 300 points. If you pay everything on time, your credit score is automatically going to be 493 (300 + 193 for paying everything on time). Then let's say you've borrowed half of your available credit. That's going to give you half of the possible 163 points for that factor, so we'll call that 80 points. That's going to bring your score up to 573 (493 + 80). Now, if you're paying everything on time and you're borrowing money, you obviously have some credit with some age, but let's say the average age of your credit is just five years, which is half of the "perfect" age of ten years. You'll get half of the possible 83 points available there, which will bring your score up to 613 (573 + 40). Then let's say you have one credit card and a car loan and that's it. No personal loan, no mortgage—just those two lines of credit. You'll probably qualify for half of the possible 55 points for types of credit, so we'll just call that 25 points. That's going to bring your score up to 638 (573 + 25).

Can you get a mortgage with a credit score of 638? Absolutely!

That's not even accounting for the other 55 points you can get from having no inquiries. Let's say you have five inquiries on your credit—another 25-point dent on your credit—you're still sitting at 668 points (638+30). That's not perfect credit by any means, but it's going to get you some loans.

This example is a pretty average snapshot of the average person's credit score. You can now look at each of those factors and see how you can manipulate any single one of them.

Now that I know the truth about credit scores, I can guarantee that my credit score will never go below 700 because of two reasons:

First, I never make a late payment. Period.

Second, I keep my borrowed balances between zero and 20 percent of my $660,000. That makes a big difference. Those two things alone will keep my score at 700 or above.

Now, all that being said, I need to tell you a very important truth: there's a good chance your credit score doesn't matter. Think about it. If you aren't trying to buy a house or a car with a bank loan, your credit score is irrelevant anyway. So many people are concentrating on rebuilding their credit score as some kind of mark of their self-worth Let me assure you, your credit score is not your self-worth. Don't worry about your credit score unless you are going to use it in the very near future.

It's that simple. Once you understand how all of this works, you don't have to play the game anymore. You are no longer a victim of the false information being circulated out there. You are free to become a master of your own credit score, your own future, and to win the game on your terms.

CHAPTER 8

Rebuilding Your Credit Using Credit Cards

When I went bankrupt, I lost everything. When something like that happens on that kind of scale, most people don't really know what to do next. They don't know how to start over—how to recover and rebuild. They are paralyzed by uncertainty, so they just sit in the financial ashes of their past mistakes. For me, I knew exactly what I needed to do. I had to immediately begin rebuilding my credit, starting that same day.

I left bankruptcy court with my discharge paper and went straight to the Toyota dealership to buy a car. The guy ran my credit and paused. Then he looked up at me and said, "Your credit score is 420."

"I know," I said. (I thought it was going to be worse, actually.)

"Well, I can still get you a loan, but the interest rate is going to be high. Are you okay with paying 24 percent interest on your car?"

I laughed. "I just walked away from $3 million of debt. I don't care about paying 24 percent interest on a loan."

So, he wrote up the deal, and I drove away in a new pre-owned car.

I didn't even need the car. But I knew what I was doing. I knew I had to establish credit immediately. So, I bought a $10,000 car at 24 percent interest. If I would have run the loan for the entire four years, that $10,000 car would have cost me almost $16,000. I had no intention of doing that. I planned on paying the loan off within the next six months, and I did. Three years later—just thirty-six months after filing for bankruptcy—I bought another car at 8.5 percent interest.

Yeah, I knew what I was doing.

I still do.

It's been more than ten years since I made that decision. Today, when I pull my wallet out of my pocket, I am holding $660,000 in the palm of my hand. I was able to rebuild my credit so well that I'm not only buying tons of real estate again, but I can charge over half a million dollars on credit cards alone. Do you realize how powerful that is? I want you to. In fact, I want you to have that same opportunity yourself.

I am going to teach you some of the strategies I used to get where I am today. But I have to warn you that what I'm going to tell you might pinch a little bit because it's going to be the complete opposite of everything you've ever been told. The truth is that the true rules of the game are not the rules you've been learning your whole life.

Credit Cards

Anyone with a credit score below 600 still has the opportunity to get it into normal range. The answer is to apply for credit cards. It takes credit to get credit. Everyone tells you not to do that, I know—but you can tune out 99 percent of those people because they're broke. Don't listen to broke people!

The other one percent understands that they're talking to the other 99. Pundits such as Dave Ramsey say that you should never have a credit balance and that you should be working to lower your balance on credit cards every month. George S. Clason, the author of *Richest Man in Babylon*, taught that you should put 20 percent of your income towards paying off your debts. I even preach that same principle in my first book! Have I changed my mind since I wrote that book? No. Generally speaking, I agree that credit cards shouldn't be put into the hands of the average American who's doing average American things.

Credit cards in and of themselves are not the problem. The problem is that most people tend to use them wrong and in the worst ways possible. Credit cards become a problem when people view them as extra income. The promise of getting what they want right now overrides their common sense, and they end up paying a big price for their greed later.

However, there are some exceptions to these rules, and I firmly believe that credit cards have their place. They are a valuable tool for both personal and business expenses. A healthy line of credit can keep your family or business financially afloat for a long time in periods of financial trouble. They can be leveraged to improve and to preserve your financial life.

How to Get Credit Cards

So, how do you start building your credit empire? By taking your first step and getting that first line of credit. When I went bankrupt, I didn't have a line of creditors lining up to give me credit cards. No, it took me a while. My first credit card after my bankruptcy had a $500 limit, and that was two years after my bankruptcy.

Before that, all I had was a debit card. Sometimes I would have to pay for an expensive dinner for my clients, and I would have to go to my boss and ask him to advance me some money so I could cover it. It was so embarrassing. He understood, and he'd always give me the advance, but that wasn't the point. It was really hard not having a credit card—not having the ability to manage my cash flow in situations like that.

When I got my first credit card, I was careful to use it responsibly. A year later, the credit card company raised my limit to $750. The thing about credit is that once you have some, it's easier to get more. It wasn't long before I was able to get a second and then a third card. Within four years, I built up my available credit to about $10,000. A few more years after that, I had $30,000 available to me. Three years after that, I had over *$500,000* available to me. Yes, it took me just three years to move my available credit from $30,000 to $500,000. You can do it, too.

Remember: It takes credit to get credit.

The types of credit cards I apply for are Visa, MasterCard, and Discover only. American Express is okay, but that company usually charges an annual fee. I am opposed to annual fees, as I believe the credit card companies make enough off of people like me as it is. If your credit score is damaged, however, you may need to pay an annual fee for your credit card. For the most part, I believe you should agree to pay those fees as an effort to rebuild your credit score. Within time, however, you will repair your credit enough that you can cancel your fee-based cards and use others.

At the moment, I have two fee-based credit cards. Both of them have a fee of $99 a year, but my credit limits are $25,000 and $40,000. The $99 is worth it—I'll pay it for that kind of credit line. That's about what it will take to get me to pay it, though. None of my other cards have any fees. And I have a *lot* of other cards. I use an Excel spreadsheet to manage and keep track of them all because it has gotten so crazy.

Here's another tip that will help you out a lot: When you're applying and you're asked how much you make per year, I want you to change your mind on how much money you make. Most people answer that question with how much they made last year. That's the most short-sighted answer I've ever heard, especially for entrepreneurs. Doesn't everyone expect to make more money this year than they did last year? If you made $80,000 last year, but this year you expect to make $150,000, why are you putting down $80,000? No—write down $150,000. Put down what you expect to make this year. That will help you out during the application process.

You have to be wise on the flip side, too, though. When I started to make really interesting six-figure numbers, I was pretty proud to put those numbers down on my application. Then they started asking me for my tax returns. I figured out that anything I reported over $300,000 would flip that switch. Now, I have to lower the numbers of my actual income on my applications. I just write in "$280,000" across the board. I suggest you do the same if you're in that boat.

The *Wrong* Type of Credit

All that being said, however, there are still only certain types of credit cards you should get. For instance, I advise that you should never get a department store credit card. If your credit ceiling is $5,000 and $2,000 of that is dedicated to department stores, that only leaves you with $3,000 for your needs. If your heater breaks in the middle of the winter, will the repairman take a Macy's credit card to fix it? I think not. No, department store credit cards are a waste of your available credit.

My clients often ask, "Isn't it easier to get a department store credit card first, and then I can use that to build my credit?" The answer is no to both! It is actually harder to get a department store credit card, as the default rate is higher. As for using it to build your credit, it actually hurts your ability to get the kind of credit you will need when you need it.

You also want to make sure that you're only securing revolving accounts. If they are not revolving—if you can't reuse them when you pay them back—don't touch them. You want a credit line you can use again and again once you pay it back.

How Much Credit Should You Have?

Once my clients understand the importance of credit cards, their next question is, "How many credit cards should I have?" My answer is that you should have as many credit cards as you can get.

If you keep applying for and getting approved for credit cards, you will eventually hit a ceiling of available credit that lenders will feel comfortable giving you. This ceiling depends on credit scores, demographics, and other key factors. If you're committed to being responsible with your credit, you want to be at your ceiling of available credit at all times. I often apply for credit even though I know

I will probably be turned down because why not? I'm already at my ceiling, but sometimes the creditor surprises me and gives me another credit card or raises my limit.

You should always ask your existing lenders for higher limits because the more credit you have, the higher your credit score will be (as long as you don't misuse your credit). If you ask your lender and they say no, big deal. You aren't any worse off than you were before, and you can always ask again later. But if they say yes, then you just got yourself some more credit. Even if they do raise your limit, you still want to ask again later. I have a Discover card with a $19,400 limit that started out as $600. Do you think I only asked to have it raised one time? No way. So, you want to keep asking, over and over again.

I can now access over $660,000 on credit cards. How many times have I asked to up my limit to get to that point? A heck of a lot. How many no's do you think I've heard? A heck of a lot! I can probably get more no's in a day than most people get in a year. But who cares? I have applied for more credit cards in the last month than you probably have in your entire life. What percentage of no's do you think I got compared to the number of times I asked? I'm going to say it was close to 97 percent. And I have still increased my available credit by $35,000 in about two months. (The funniest rejection letter I got was from Barclays Bank. I applied to raise my credit limit from $40,000 to $60,000. The letter I received said, "We are denying your increase in credit because you are aggressively seeking credit." I laughed hysterically when I read that. Talk about an understatement!)

It doesn't matter how bad your credit is or what the credit card company says they will or will not do today. Nothing's been done that can't be undone.

Before I filed for bankruptcy, I had three American Express cards. When I went bankrupt, they took all my American Express cards—I lost all of my lines of credit everywhere I had them; that's how it works. Well, American Express has a rule that if you lose your Amex card through bankruptcy, you will never be allowed to have one again. The fine print of the Amex application actually says "never." That's fine with me—I don't aspire to have a card with that company. I am getting credit all the time, so it's not like I need one. Well, have you ever noticed that when you order on Amazon that you can get an Amazon credit card that you can use for cash back on all of your purchases? I order on Amazon all the time—it's like Christmas every day—so, when I saw that ad for 5 percent cash back with an Amazon credit card, I immediately clicked on it to apply.

I filled out the application, and the next screen said, "Thank you for applying to American Express." I rolled my eyes and regretted wasting five minutes of my life on that. Then suddenly, the next thing I knew, the screen said, "Congratulations! You've been approved for a $2,500 line of credit!" I was amazed! I wanted to see how far I could push it. I logged into my account immediately and asked for an increase. To my surprise, I got another $500 on the spot.

I got $3,000 from a company that swore it would never give me a card ever again.

A couple months later, I was buying cubicles for my office and the cubicle company wanted a $2,500 deposit. I wanted to put it on my American Express card and get that 5 percent cash back, but I already had a $700 balance on my card. I needed to make some room. I could have just paid off that $700, but again, I wanted to see how far I could push the envelope. Instead of paying off my balance, I applied for an increase on my card. The application has a place where you can type in how much you want. I wrote $7,500. They gave it to me. They more than doubled my line of credit! I should have asked for $15,000—maybe I would've gotten it. I only put $7,500 for kicks because I was certain the company was going to say no. I guess I'll know better next time—and there will definitely be a next time.

Won't This Hurt Your Credit Score?

You may wonder how all of this will affect your credit score. Yes, the first ten inquiries are going to affect you. Each inquiry will give a small hit to your score, which will last two years. However, if your available credit increases, your credit score will go up. That means that if you're approved for the credit, your inquiry decrease will be offset by your credit increase. Who cares if you get dinged three points on your credit score for an inquiry if it means you could get approved and bring up your score by thirty points? It's normal for my students to see their credit scores jump by fifty points or more within their first month of coaching with me, and that's mostly because they're following my advice and securing more credit.

More important, you need to understand that, for the most part, your on-hand available credit is more useful than your credit score. Isn't that the point of having a good credit score in the first place? So you can get credit when you need it? Your credit score is not your life worth. It's just a number—a number that predicts whether or not you'll make a late payment in the next ninety days.

I would rather have the credit available to me when I don't need it then be so overly cautious about my credit score that I end up getting turned down for credit when I do. Look at it this way: Would you rather have a credit score of 520 and $500,000 of available credit on your credit cards, or a credit score of 810 and $30,000 available on your credit cards? That should be an easy question to answer. If you have more available credit than you could ever need, who cares what your credit score is? You *are* the bank! Unless you're buying your primary residence or buying a car, your credit score is irrelevant.

So, apply, apply, apply!

When to STOP Applying for Credit

There is a very important exception to this rule, though. You should never apply for credit between the time you put in an offer on the house that you are going to live in—your primary residence only—and the time you close. That's the only time you silence your inquiries. I've had many clients lose the ability to buy a house because they applied for credit at the same time they were trying to buy a house. Only apply for mass credit cards at least six months before you are considering a mortgage—then feel free to start applying again the day after you close.

How To Use (and Not Use) Your Credit

As you start to accumulate credit cards, it's important that you keep your greed in check. Remember that these lines of credit are not meant to be pay days. They are resources that can be leveraged to get you where you want to go. Never lose sight of the strategy. If you do, things can get really messy really fast.

The first rule of using credit cards is that they should never be used to buy the things that you want. Credit should only be used to buy things you need. When I say this to my clients, I have found that many of them don't really understand the difference between a want and a need. This is how I define them: A "need" is something you absolutely cannot live without. A "want" is something you can live without.

Here is where it gets fuzzy. Let's say your car is in the shop and the tech says it needs a new engine. If your car is really old, well—it's time for a new car. You probably won't have the cash to buy the new car, so you'll have to use credit for your purchase. (But if you do have the cash on hand, there's still a best way to make that purchase. See *Chapter 10: The Right Way to Buy a Car.*)

The car is definitely a need.

The *type* of car you choose is a want.

You should never buy a car with a purchase price of more than 25 percent of your annual income. If you're making $50,000 a year, you shouldn't buy a car for more than $12,500. You probably know some people who have purchased cars worth more than their entire annual income. I promise you, it's not worth it. You might enjoy that luxury for a short season, but it won't last. That is a sure way to the poor house.

When you're looking at purchasing a new car—a legitimate need—find a car that fits your income parameters. You need to have a car that will drive you to work and allow you to live a productive life. You don't need to impress yourself and your friends with a shiny BMW. That's a want.

The same goes for basics such as food, furniture, and clothes. You need these things in order to live your life. However, you don't need to dine at five-star restaurants, sit on Italian leather, or wear Armani suits all the time. I'm not saying these are bad things or that you shouldn't have them. Personally, I love these kinds of luxuries! I'm just saying that they aren't needs and should therefore never show up on your credit card statements. Your wants should always be paid for with cash-on-hand funds.

That being said, you may eventually cross a new threshold where you decide to use your credit cards for all of your purchases for the sake of perks such as travel miles or cash back. In that event, your plan should be to pay off those charges with your cash-on-hand funds immediately. Don't ever let them accumulate as credit on your accounts. Just think of those purchases as a two-step process: one swipe with your credit card, then a debit transaction to pay it off.

If you use your lines of credit correctly and wisely, they can help grow those cash-on-hand funds. For instance, as a real estate entrepreneur, I have Home Depot and Lowe's credit cards. I use them for when I am renovating houses and could use a short-term materials loan at 0 percent interest. This is just good business. Using credit cards this way allows me to leverage my assets and increase my overall income faster. There are so many ways credit cards can be used to help you reach your financial goals faster.

Once you learn the rules of how things really work, everything changes. In the next chapter, I'm going to blow your mind with exactly what's possible.

CHAPTER 9

LLCs: The Credit Multiplier

After reading the last chapter, are you feeling a little skeptical? When I tell people I have over $660,000 available to me in credit cards, I usually get one of two responses: Either they don't believe me at all, or they do believe me, but they don't believe it's possible for them.

It's definitely possible for you, but you have to be willing to go against the grain a little bit. You have to be willing to step outside of your comfort zone and unlearn a lot of the things that you've been taught about credit and financial strategies.

By now, you're probably thinking, *What's the catch, Larry? Just tell me what it is.* There is no catch. But there is a set of specific strategies you need to follow. If you're in real estate, this may be especially hard for you to swallow because I'm teaching you things completely backwards from the way you've already learned them. Seriously, real estate agents are the hardest people for me to talk to because I have got to unteach them everything they know. If you're in that boat, I assure you that I know what I'm talking about. I am licensed to teach the licensing course, and I am a broker. You can rely on my experience.

The Piece That Makes This Work

In the last chapter, I told you that you need to start accumulating credit by applying for credit. I told you that you need to ask for higher limits and manage your credit responsibly. All of that is completely true. There's a piece to all of this that I haven't told you yet, though, and that is the piece that makes all of this work. Are you ready? Here it is:

You have to start building credit in your business name. I am currently holding in my wallet over half a million dollars-worth of credit cards. If you look at each card, one by one, you will see that not all of them are issued to Larry Steinhouse.

Do you currently have an LLC or an S Corp? If not, it doesn't take long to set one up. You could have it up and going by the end of the week, if not the day. I encourage you to do this. (If you are an employee going to work eight hours a day, this doesn't apply to you as much—but since you're reading this book, I'm going to go out on a limb and assume you're an entrepreneur.)

We do classes at InvestorSchooling.com on how to apply for LLCs, but here's a quick tutorial: Once you get your EIN number, you want to go to Dun & Bradstreet at DNB.com and get a DUNS number. You have heard of Equifax, Transunion, etc.—the companies who rank your credit. Well, Dun & Bradstreet ranks business credit, which is different from personal credit. This DUNS number is important to have because when you apply for credit, the first thing the lender does is look for your DUNS number. So basically, once you have the DUNS number, you become a real company.

There are many advantages to having an LLC, and one of my favorites is that it gives you an avenue for securing more credit. Now, if your credit score isn't great at the moment, opening an LLC isn't going to change that. Some people believe they're going to open an LLC and magically get credit when their own credit score is 500. That just isn't going to happen. However, as you work to improve your credit score following the strategies I outlined to you in the last couple chapters, you can multiply the doors that will open to you by having an LLC.

Building Business Credit

Once you open your LLC, begin to establish credit there as quickly as possible. If your credit score is decent, I suggest purchasing your next vehicle in the name of your LLC. Do not buy it in your name. You are going to pay more insurance when you do it this way, but it's worth it. Once you've established that loan in your business name, it will be easy to get credit cards in your business name. You will apply, and you will get them.

The other big bonus here is that even though you will have to personally guarantee the loan, the loan itself will not show up on your personal credit report. This is because the LLC is a separate legal entity from you. It has a different identification number—an EIN number—outside of your social security number, so it's not going to be connected to your personal credit at all. This is a good thing. Not only will you be establishing a credit history for your LLC, but you won't be putting any pressure on your personal debt-to-income ratio. That's important because, generally speaking, the more personal debt you have, the less new credit you will be approved for.

For instance, if you walk into a bank trying to get a mortgage for a home and the bank pulls your credit report and sees that you have a $700 car loan on there, that's going to hurt you. The bank looks at your debt-to-income ratio to determine how much you can afford to pay for your mortgage. If you have that $700 car loan in your LLC's name, however, it's not going to show up on your personal credit report at all. It's as if it doesn't exist.

Also, remember that I told you that 165 points of your credit score are based on how much of your available credit is being used. At the time of this writing, I have five companies, all of which have credit and assets. If I'm only using those lines of credit, how much debt does Larry Steinhouse have? Zero dollars. How many points are my lines of credit shaving off of my credit score? Zero points. I keep all 165 of them. My LLCs could cumulatively owe the credit card companies $100,000, and it still wouldn't show up on my personal credit report—the very credit report that is being used to determine how much credit I am issued in any new LLCs I may open.

That's powerful.

Right now, Larry Steinhouse owns nothing. I have multiple investment properties, but how many of them are in my name? None. I drive a Corvette Z06 worth $100,000, a Mercedes SL550 worth $150,000, a Ford 150 Lariat worth $60,000, and a Jeep Cherokee worth $48,000. How many of those do I own? None. My companies own all of them.

I'm also in the market for a Mustang. I know exactly what I'm looking for. Let's say I find it and then go to get a loan for that car.

If the bank pulls up my credit report and sees I'm paying $5,000 a month in car payments, is the bank going to give me a loan? No way. The trick is that I've got $5,000 worth of car payments no one sees. If you look at my debt-to-income ratio, I have no debt. I owe a lot of money, but I have no personal debt.

When I went to buy the Corvette, the dealer asked, "Are you going to finance this?"

"I don't know," I said. "Can I put it in my company name?"

"Of course," he said. "How much do you want to put down?"

"How much do I have to put down?"

"Nothing."

"Let me get this straight," I said. "You are going to give me a $100,000 car and let me drive away without giving you a dime?"

"Yes, sir. You won't have to make your first payment for thirty days."

America—what an amazing place! My mind was completely blown.

Now, do you think that would have been the case if he would have pulled my credit report and seen multiple car payments on there? I think not.

More Companies, More Credit

One of my LLCs—we'll call it ABC Properties LLC—owns four cars, has a bunch of credit cards, and has a great credit score. It's exactly where I want it to be. So, now I need to build another LLC. And then another, and another, and another. I currently have five companies, but that number is going to continue to go up. One of my businesses has over $150,000 worth of credit available. That's just one of my businesses. Most people don't even have that much personal credit available to them. I'm not trying to say that I'm any better than the next guy in anyway. I just want you to understand what is possible for you. Each LLC becomes another invisible arm of your investment power. My advice is to do this as many times as possible. Always get credit while you can.

LLCs Protect Your Personal Credit

I build out these LLCs because, number one, it keeps all my investments out of my personal name. Doing this also builds a silo of future financial security. What will happen to me if my personal credit goes to crap? It's not likely going to happen—I've learned the lessons I need to in order to keep that from happening again—but what if? Well, I still have multiple companies with great credit. I will still have power to purchase and invest. If I mess up my credit, that disaster stays self-contained and can't hurt the other arms of my credit.

I'm safe.

Be careful, though, because that doesn't work both ways. For example, I have a truck owned by ABC Properties LLC, but I've had to personally guarantee that loan. If ABC Properties doesn't make the payments, Larry Steinhouse is responsible for that debt. Ford will come back to me and hold me accountable for that loan. If I don't take care of it, it's going to hurt my personal credit.

Asset Protection for You and Your Family

Now, let's say that, for some reason, you're not worried about building business credit and you just want to buy everything with cash—you still want to put your assets in your LLCs or in trusts. It's a simple matter of protection. It won't make you bullet-proof, but you will be awfully close. If something does happen and someone goes after you, you will have all of your assets safely tucked away into different entities. No one will be able to touch them.

I'm not saying that you are going to do anything wrong, but life happens. You can't foresee every misfortune that could come your way. For instance, you may have an elderly relative go into a nursing home. Then all of a sudden, Medicaid wants to know what assets that person has. Medicaid will deduct the value of your loved one's assets from that person's Medicaid benefits. Now, let's say you knew this was going to happen. You saw it coming six months ahead of time because your elderly relative was declining in health and would soon need twenty-four-hour care. So, you counseled your loved one to sell her rental property to you or to a friend or somebody else because you thought you were a genius and you were protecting her assets from Medicaid. Wrong. Medicaid does a 5-year lookback. They will say, "Hey, you recently sold that property and got $200,000 for it. We are going to take $200,000 off your Medicaid benefit."

This really happens. I know people it has happened to. So, it's best not to own anything, if at all possible. When the time comes and Medicaid ever does a lookback on me, there is literally nothing to see. All of my properties are in trusts, owned by a piece of paper. I happen to be the trustee, of course, but they are all owned by a piece of paper. They're not in my name. If anything happens to me and I've got to go into a nursing home, at any age—this age, tomorrow, ten years from now—I don't own anything except my primary residence, which, by the way, is untouchable if my spouse is living there.

By the way, my primary residence is also in a trust. Not only that, but when I die, the beneficiaries of my trusts are my LLCs. You're probably thinking, *Larry, what about your children?* Well, I actually did this for my kids. You see, I don't want them paying out half of their inheritances in taxes. I don't care if you are Democrat or Republican. You still don't want the IRS to take most of the money you saved up.

So, here's the twist: the beneficiaries of my trusts are my LLCs. I currently own my LLCs, but I am about to gift my LLCs to my children. The LLCs themselves do not own any properties. They're just shells. So, I'm basically gifting my children nothing at this point. While I am alive, I will still be the trustee of these trusts, and therefore the controller of all of my properties—even once my children own the LLCs. The properties won't actually go into the LLCs until I die. And when I do, the beneficiaries—the LLCs that my children own—get all the properties, and that is how my children will own them. From a tax standpoint, on paper, they never did not own them. Therefore, there is no inheritance tax.

So, you see—having multiple LLCs isn't just about investing smart. It's about living smart, too. When you do things this way, you are literally structuring your wealth in the best way possible for generations to come.

CHAPTER 10

The Right Way to Buy a Car

Okay, I hope by now we can all agree that you need to have your LLC buy your next vehicle. Now let's talk about the smartest way to do that.

Have you ever heard of a one-pay lease? If you have, you're in the minority of people on this planet. Most people have not—and that's no accident. The car industry doesn't want you to know about it. That's because anything that saves you money is keeping your dollars out of their pockets. They don't like that. But here, I'm going to tell you all about it and how to make it work for you.

The True Cost of a Used Car

As a real estate investor, I do a lot of wholesaling—also known as contract reassignment. What is that? It's like this: Say Chris has a house for sale, and he sells it to me for $50,000. Now, once I've either purchased the house or have it under contract, I can take that contract and sell it to Bob for $60,000 and make $10,000 right out of the gate. This is wholesaling, and I love those deals. I can make a lot of money doing very little work.

I used to have people going out and doing those deals for me. They'd find the houses and handle the transactions. But at this point, I like going out and doing some of the deals myself. I love the thrill of it—it's one of the reasons I got into this business in the first place. Now, a lot of these deals are made on the side of town where I'm not going to ride through in my Corvette Z06. If I do, the person I'm trying to make a deal with isn't going to be very motivated to take my offer. He'll take one look at my car then shake his head and ask me for more money. And then I'm not sure I will come back and find my wheels still attached to my car. (The wheels are probably worth more than some of the houses in the area!)

So, I bought a beater car for my "business trips" into downtown Philly. At the time, I had $10,000 that I'd allocated to buy an SUV. I'm going to tell you exactly how I spent that money to get the most car for my dollars.

First, let's talk about what that ten grand can get you if you're buying a used SUV. Let's say you find a 2017 Nissan Sentra with 32,000 miles on it and it is being sold for $9,900 (this is based on a real search result). Most of you probably have—or have had—cars with 32,000 miles on it. At that point, you need a tune-up, which is going to cost you about $350. Then you're going to need to replace the breaks and tires, which will be another $1,000. Even if your car doesn't need these things today, you can guarantee that sometime within the next three years, you will. It's also going to come out of warranty during that time.

So, fast forward three years after your purchase. Your mileage will probably be somewhere around 62,000 or so, and the vehicle will be out of warranty. You'll probably have spent $3,000 to $4,000 on maintenance during that three-year period. And is it going to have a nice, new-car smell? No. It will be more like the "fifty people" smell (if you've ever bought a used car, you know what I'm talking about.)

After just thirty-six months, that $10,000 beater has now become a $13,000 to $14,000 money pit that is still depreciating in value. You will never recoup that investment. It's money out the window. I didn't want to do that. So, I didn't.

The One-Pay Lease

Instead of going that route, I went to a Hyundai dealer and bought a brand-new Tucson. Only, I didn't buy it. I leased it.

I leased a brand-new Hyundai Tucson that had a sticker price of $27,000. The one-pay lease on this car was $9,300. It came with a 36,000-mile warranty and free oil changes for the lifetime of the lease. How much did I have to put into that car over the next three years? Nothing. Zero dollars in maintenance costs.

And by the way, if I'd gone for a month-to-month lease, it would have cost me over $10,000. The monthly payment plus the interest rate would have been about $284 each month. That comes to a total of $10,224 after the three years is up. By paying the entire lease upfront, I shaved off about $25 in interest every month, which saved me more than $900 on the over-all lease transaction alone.

Why buy a used car with your cash when you could be driving a brand-new car for less?

Lease the Car in Your Business' Name

When you do this, you can—and should!—put the car in the name of your LLC. This is a great way to build credit for your company.

How many cars do you think I own? I've already mentioned just a couple of the cars I drive right here in this chapter. Some of the cars I drive are a Mercedes SL550, a Jeep Cherokee, a Ford F150—and then there's my Harley Davidson. But here's the catch: I don't own any of them. Larry Steinhouse owns zero cars. Which is the same number of houses I own. (See *Chapter 9: LLCs—The Credit Multiplier* for more information on how LLCs can increase your buying power and protect you financially.) I control all of them, but I don't own any of them.

When I went to lease the Tucson, I had one LLC with about $150,000 in credit, another one with $30,000 in credit, and then I had a new company that had none. I wanted to build up some business credit in that third business, so I did the one-pay lease option and put the car in my business' name. Remember, that was a business that had no credit at the time. Would I have been able to buy a car in the name of that LLC? No way. I wouldn't even have been able to get approved for the regular thirty-six-month lease. But how hard do you think it is to get approved for a lease when you're paying the whole thing off on the same day? It's pretty easy.

You might be thinking this deal isn't going to build any credit because it is a one-pay deal. But that's not true. The dealer still has to go through the approval process to get you approved, and then it opens up an account in your company name. That credit account is going to be open for three years with a zero balance. So, now that new LLC has a car in its name, it has credit, and the LLC's DUNS number now reflects that it has a line of credit and that it's being paid on time.

How the One-Pay Lease Saves You Money

Some of you may be thinking, *Why lease a car when you could own it? Leasing is like paying on a car forever.*

But even if you plan on buying a car, doing the one-pay lease upfront can still save you money and protect you from getting upside down on your loan. Let me break it down for you. For this example, we'll use a brand-new Tucson with a sticker price of $27,000. What else do you have to pay for when you purchase a new car? Sales tax. In Philadelphia, that's going to be 6 percent of the purchase price, so $1,620. That brings the total purchase price to $28,620, if I paid for it in cash.

If you lease the car instead, you will pay $9,300 up front. Then, there's something called a residual value. This is the purchase price the dealer agrees to extend to you for your vehicle when your lease is up; it's in your lease agreement. The residual value on this car happened to be $17,500. If you add that to the one-pay lease price, it comes to $26,800, and you'd only have to pay the sales tax on the $17,500, which would be $1,050. The difference in sales tax alone, when compared to buying the car new, would be a credit to you of $570.

So, let's look at the numbers: It would have been $28,620 to buy the car outright, plus you would have been responsible for maintaining the vehicle. Instead, you pay $9,300 and have no monthly payments or maintenance fees for three years. If you decide to keep the car after that, the total purchase price—including the lease amount and the sales tax—would be $27,850. That's a difference of $770.

But that's only if you decide to keep it.

What if the car is still worth $19,000 at the end of your lease? You could purchase the car and resell it and make a quick profit of $1,500. But what if the market value is less than the contract amount? In that case, you can just hand it back to the dealer and say, "I'll come back and get it once it's on the lot and priced at $15,000." That happens a lot, by the way. So, it doesn't matter what the car is worth at the end of your lease. You still save money in every scenario. You can't go wrong. (And of course, you can always just walk away from the deal altogether and go lease another car, which is what I like to do.)

Finally, let's say you really do have the money to pay for the car outright today. Maybe you want to do that so that you can avoid getting a loan and paying interest. But compare the initial cash investment of $9,300 to $28,620. At first glance, that might seem like an irrelevant comparison. Afterall, in one scenario you're just leasing the car and in the other you outright own it. It's apples to oranges, right? Wrong. The difference between those two numbers today is $19,320. Imagine what you could do with that money in thirty-six months! I can think of a hundred ways I could double that money is three years. Why tie it up in a vehicle when you can invest it into an asset that can pay for that car?

That is the power of a one-pay lease.

CHAPTER 11

How to Buy a House with Credit Cards

Once you truly get these concepts and you're building your available credit and you're leveraging the power of LLCs, you will be amazed by what is possible.

I'm a real estate investor, and I routinely use these concepts to buy properties without using banks. Of all the properties I have bought in the last ten years, I've only used a bank to buy one of them. *One*. That's it. That was also the only time I had to reveal my credit score. If you're not using a bank, then your credit score is irrelevant.

How is this done, you ask? Well, have you ever heard of buying a house with a credit card? No? You're in for a surprise then.

Imagine you're a real estate investor and you find a house priced at $250,000. You inspect the property and determine it needs about $50,000 of repairs, and its after-repair value, or ARV, will be $500,000. If you can just come up with the $300,000 to make it happen, you can make a quick $200,000. It's a great deal you don't want to pass up. The problem is you already have a home loan, a car loan, and $80,000 of credit available to you in credit cards. You've maxed out your credit opportunities. There's no bank in the world that's going to give you the money to buy this house. Even if the bank did give you a loan, it's not going to cover the whole thing. You'd be lucky to get 80 percent of the purchase price.

You're not going to walk away from this deal, though. So, what do you do?

First, you're going to go to a hard-money lender. He's not going to pull your credit report. He doesn't care about that. All he cares about is the viability of your investment and how much money you are coming up with out of pocket to make it happen. A hard money lender will usually give you 70 percent of the purchase price plus money for the repairs. In this case, you could expect the full $50,000 for the repairs and 70 percent of purchase price, which would be $175,000. That gives you a total of $225,000 toward the $300,000 you need to buy the property.

How are you going to come up with the other $75,000?

Well, you have those credit cards just sitting there with $80,000 on them. But how can you liquidate that credit into the cash that you need? There are two ways you could typically do this. First, some credit cards will allow you to write a check to yourself. This isn't a bad idea, especially if you have zero percent checks—sometimes that happens—but you will typically be charged a 4 percent fee on any checks you write. The problem with writing the check, however, is that it takes ten days to clear, and you might not have ten days before closing. In order for it to work, you have to write the check about two weeks ahead of time.

The other way is to get a cash advance. The problem with a cash advance, though, is that it's the worst possible option. For one, it's extremely expensive. There is a higher rate of interest on cash advances. Second, you will only be able to take a portion of your available credit as a cash advance. Let's say you have a $10,000 limit. You'd probably only be able to pull out about $3,500 in cash.

Well, now I want to tell you about a third option. You've probably heard of this little company called PayPal, right? If you don't already have a PayPal account, get one right now. Then, I want you to open one in your business name. I'm serious—if you don't already have one in your business name, I challenge you to open one by the end of the day. Once you do that—once you have two separate PayPal accounts functioning as two separate entities—you can send yourself a bill of services. In my case, ABC Properties LLC would send Larry Steinhouse a bill for services totaling $75,000. Then, I'm going to take three or four different credit cards and pay that bill in full. Larry Steinhouse is left with four different credit card bills of varying amounts. ABC Properties is left with a lump sum of $75,000, which it will promptly use to go buy a house.

When you do it this way, I still recommend that you use your LLC credit cards to pay the bill so that the transactions don't show up on your personal credit report.

If you want to get really crazy, and you have the room for it on your credit cards, you can put the entire balance of the house on your credit cards this way. Yes, PayPal is going to charge you about 3 percent on that transaction, but who cares? It's less than you're going to pay using a credit card check and way less than you're going to pay getting a cash advance from your credit card. That 3 percent will be money saved and money well spent.

But wait—there's more!

PayPal Credit

PayPal also offers credit, which comes with six months free financing on everything. I have multiple PayPal Credit accounts—one for myself and each of my businesses. One of my companies has $10,000 in available PayPal Credit, and another has $7,500.

When you first open your PayPal Credit line, you're not going to have $10,000 right out of the gate. But if you're careful and you're patient, it will get there. When I first opened my PayPal Credit account a few years after my bankruptcy, I was offered $400 for six months, interest free. The way I've gotten my credit line so high is that I've found that you can generally purchase a bit more than your limit and then PayPal automatically increases your limit to that number. When I had a $400 limit, I charged it up to $450 and then that became my new limit. Then I charged that up to $500 and that became my new limit. Then I charged it up to $600, which became my new limit, and so on and so forth. I did this for years until I got it all the way up to $10,000. That seems to be the limit because I haven't been able to charge it any higher than that.

You see, I sit around and devise ways to get more credit just for fun. I swear it has become an obsession. You get to reap the benefits of my obsession, though, so you're welcome.

Now, once I've worked my system for multiple LLCs, let's say ABC Properties sends Investor Schooling an invoice for $10,000, and then Investor Schooling pays that bill with PayPal Credit. I just created $10,000 of free money for six months! It never even shows up on my credit report, even if it's in my personal name. PayPal doesn't report credit activities to the credit bureaus.

I'm not just interested in that $10,000 of free money, though. I'm looking way ahead of that. What if I'm sending a $10,000 bill to multiple LLCs? I can create tens of thousands of dollars of free money for half a year. How long will it take me to flip that house? Can I do it in six months or less? You bet I can.

I don't recommend that you tap out all of the PayPal Credit lines among your LLCs, though, because you want to keep an ace in the hole. Let me explain: if Investor Schooling doesn't have the money to pay its $10,000 loan in six months, then Investor Schooling can send an invoice for $10,000 to one of my other companies, and then that company will pay the bill using PayPal Credit, and now I've rolled that $10,000 over into another six-month period at zero percent interest. With multiple PayPal accounts, I can keep doing this every six months for quite a while. You just have to be sure to keep a credit line open at all times so that you have the capacity to roll it over.

This is a powerful strategy if you apply it correctly. Let me repeat that: This is a powerful strategy *if* you apply it correctly. If you don't manage this right, you are going to get yourself into some big trouble. I'm not talking about laws. If you are not paying attention and paying all of these things on time, then you're going to be charged interest and a lot of these perks are going to go away. So, make sure you're managing this right! Personally, I keep a spreadsheet with all of this on it so that I can track everything that way.

That, ladies and gentleman, is how you buy houses with credit cards.

That's how you create wealth out of thin air—because you really are creating money out of thin air. If you take the money from your hard money lender and another $75,000 from your credit cards or PayPal Credit, how much money did you take out of your own pocket to buy that house? Zero dollars.

If you like that, then you're going to love the following chapters. I'm going to give you strategies for buying houses without using any of your own money—or your own credit.

CHAPTER 12

Investing With Other People's Money (OPM)

When I was younger, I used to watch shows late at night about investing with other people's money. I would think, *This is a load of crap. Who in the world would lend me money for a real estate deal?*

After I went bankrupt in 2008, I had no money and a 420 credit score. But I still wanted to buy real estate. I had no choice but to learn how to invest using OPM—other people's money.

A year and a half later, my credit score was still under 500. I bought a house with just $1,724 out of pocket. It was a two-family house with a pizzeria in it—a commercial-mix use. It is now worth over $300,000, and I have over $180,000 of equity in it. I'm taking in

$1,000 a month in profit from that deal right now. When I bought it, I was only getting $400 in profit a month, which still wasn't too bad for only putting up $1,724 of my own money for it to begin with.

Today, I make these deals all the time with zero money out of my own pocket. You can't beat that. Other People's Money is, most important, money that is not yours.

There are three primary sources of OPM:

- Banks, in the form of credit cards, home equity lines of credit (HELOC), and personal lines of credit.
- Hard money lenders
- People, in the form of IRAs, 401k plans, savings, life insurance accounts, their credit, or cash.

Banks

Banks will lend you cheap money, but it comes with a lot of red tape, and they don't like to take risks. They want to make sure you can repay them. They want to see your credit score, proof of income, and your debt-to-income ratio. If everything looks good, they still may turn you down, depending on what you're using the money for. If you do get approved, it's a painfully slow process.

However, you could go a less traditional route and use credit cards. I have about $150,000 in my wallet at all times—in the form of credit cards. I also carry blank checks connected to other lines of credit. This means I don't have to walk into a bank and ask for anything. I've already asked for it, and I'm ready to invest it when I want to.

Hard Money Lenders

Hard money lenders are the lenders who say yes when others say no.

When you use hard money lenders, you're looking at high-interest, short term loans. It's expensive money. You're looking at 12 to 16 percent interest, plus points. Points refer to the fees you have to pay up front just to get hard lenders to loan you the money. Generally, each point is equal to one percentage point of the loan. For example, if you're getting a $100,000 loan at three points, your upfront fees would be $3,000 (3 percent of $100,000).

There are two types of hard money lenders. There are the professional and the small lenders. The ones you see at trade shows with big, corporate banners—those are the professional hard money lenders. Working with them is going to be very similar to working with a bank. You're going to have a lot of paperwork. There are still guidelines and regulations you have to work around, but they don't care about your credit score. They are working based on other criteria.

The small lenders don't have the same guidelines and regulations as the professional hard money lenders. They can do more for you, and they're easier to use. They will also be a little less expensive to work with than professional hard money lenders because they don't have shareholders they have to share with or account to. However, they will only work with you if they feel like it. They make decisions at will. Even though they're easier to use, they may be harder to find.

People

People—private parties—can be the easiest lenders to work with. You're not going to have to move through a lot of red tape, and you won't have the burden of working around guidelines, regulations, and mountains of paperwork. They're not going to ask to see your credit report, paystubs, tax returns, or property appraisals. That means none of those things—or lack thereof—have the potential to screw up your deal.

It can be as easy as asking and receiving.

Finding People Who Will Give You Money

The first rule of getting investment money from other people is to ask everyone for money! Ask for money—again, and again, and again. You won't regret it. In the words of Mahatma Gandhi, "First they ignore you, then they laugh at you, then they fight you, then you win."

New people you meet: When you find yourself in a conversation with someone you just met, what's one of the first questions that comes up? "What do you do?" When someone asks you that question, your new answer is, "I raise money for incredible investment opportunities." (One of my mentors taught me this line.)

What do you think someone's going to say next? They're likely going to ask you to tell them more. "What does that mean? How does that work?" From there, you're just a few questions away from naturally being able to ask, "Do you have any money in the bank? What are you getting back from your IRA?" Boom—it goes right into it. If you start a conversation like this every time, you'll end up talking about money every time.

Mail or email your friends: You should have a list of at least 100 people who you go to anytime you're doing anything in business. I call it a wedding list. Who would you invite to a wedding? Keep that list handy at all times. Anytime you're doing something interesting—maybe it's multi-level marketing, maybe it's raising private capital—you can go to them. You can send them a letter or an email. (NOTE: You *must* know the person before you send out a letter asking for money. In most states, it's illegal to solicit money from people you don't know.)

I once found a house with a purchase price of $48,000. Repairs were estimated at $6,000, so my total upfront costs would be $54,000, and it would rent for $1,000 a month. It far surpassed the 1 percent rule, which says if a house will rent for at least 1 percent of the purchase price—including repairs—then it's probably a good deal. This house was a steal of a deal. I did a quick walk through of the property and said, "I'm taking it."

As soon as I got into my car, before I even put my seatbelt on, I texted a friend and said, "I need 60k for a deal. Interested in loaning me at 7 percent?"

She responded, "How long? Security?"

"First position on a property worth about eighty. I'm looking for five years," I said.

"Payments or interest only?"

"Either is fine."

"Tentatively yes. Please send property info and comparisons."

I got the money. I got the deal.

In the end, I asked her for $75,000 instead of $60,000. She said, "Sure, no problem." It really wasn't a problem. Why should she care? She was getting interest on every dollar she let me borrow. The more she gave me then, the more I gave her later. The only risk to her was the possibility that I wasn't going to pay her—but she already knew that wasn't a problem. I have a track record with her. She knows, likes, and trusts me. Of course, she gave me the money.

For me, this deal meant thousands of dollars at closing and a portion of the rent. Once I deducted the loan payment, I was making a positive cash flow of $275 a month. That was money in my pocket, made out of thin air. Just to give you an idea of how valuable that is, I used to label my houses: this one is my car payment, this one is my mortgage payment, and this one is my insurance payment. I'm serious. Consider your average car payment. It's somewhere around $400 dollars a month. The last time I wanted to buy a car, I bought a house so that it would pay for my car.

If You Have a Good Deal, the Money Will Find *You*

Sometimes, you don't have to find the people at all. They will find you.

I once found a duplex with a purchase price of $50,000. The repair estimate was $38,000, and once both sides were rented out, it would bring in $1,850 a month.

It's easy to see the value in this deal. The total investment would be $88,000, and the monthly rent was going to be about 2 percent of that. It was an incredible deal. (The ARV didn't matter to me because I was planning on holding the property and renting it out. But in case you're curious, it was about $150,000.)

If I took this deal to a bank, the most they would give me is $40,000. There's no way they'd give me any money to cover the repairs, and they wouldn't even give me enough to buy the house outright. Forget about renovating it. I wouldn't have the money.

But I wanted this house. I could have bought it in cash, but then I wouldn't have that cash to buy something else. I'd rather not use my cash. Well, I was at a meeting where we were all talking about our different real estate deals. I mentioned this particular deal, and afterwards, someone came up to me and said, "I want to get in on that."

I said, "Okay, lend me the money."

That person lent me $100,000. My total purchase price, plus closing costs, was about $92,000. That means I got $8,000 at closing. Once the property was repaired, it was gorgeous and rented in a second. After I deducted the $500 a month I was paying back to him on the loan, I was making a positive cashflow of $750 a month. The return on this is infinite. I paid nothing, immediately received thousands of dollars just for doing the deal, and now collect money on this property every month. It's the gift that keeps on giving.

When I did this deal, I didn't have to show him my credit score. I didn't have to have the property appraised. I didn't have to show him my W-2s or anything.

When your bank says no, say, "Thank you!"

Why Would Someone Invest in You?

Once you find potential lenders, the trick is going to be to convince them to give you money. How do you do that? Well, imagine I have a $100 bill and three people are lined up to get it. I can only choose one person to receive the entire amount. I go down the line and ask each person why they want the money.

Person number one says, "I want to take that money and go invest in real estate and start living my dream."

Person number two says, "I would like to take that money to go buy sleeping bags for the homeless."

Person number three says, "I am a mother of two children, and I need to buy diapers and Pull-Ups for my kids *today*."

Who am I going to give the money to? Person number three, of course! It's not about giving someone a handout. It's about the emotion behind the exchange. I'm investing in a woman who needs money for her children. I'm investing in a family. That feels good.

If people feel good about you and your offer—if they believe in you and your goal—it's easy to get money from them. The main thing to keep in mind is that people do business with people they know, like, and trust. If you hit all three of those markers, you're in.

That's really important for you to understand.

My brother inherited over $100,000. He called up some guy from Provincial and bought an annuity that was going to pay him 2.1 percent a year. So, he was going to get $2,100 a year, and he had to lock it in for eight years. If he wanted to take his money out sooner, he would have to pay a fee. That's because the way it works is that as soon as you pay them, the salesperson gets a 3 percent commission, which is taken out of your money. So, immediately, his account was only worth $97,000.

Then he started thinking, *I've got a brother who knows something about money. I should talk to him about this.* Good choice. So, he called me up and told me about his annuity.

I said, "Instead of doing that, give it to me and I will guarantee you 8 percent interest. You'll get $8,000 a year. I'll pay your $3,000 fee to get it out of the annuity, and I will go invest that into real estate. You won't even have to wait until the end of the year to get your return. I will start paying it to you in monthly increments immediately."

He just laughed at me. "Are you kidding me?" he asked. "You went bankrupt doing real estate ten years ago! What if that happens again?"

I went through the numbers with him and explained all the ways it wouldn't happen again. I addressed his concerns head on and gave him the information he needed in order to feel comfortable. Once I took the time to explain it to my brother, he totally got it. He trusted me.

Then, he gave me the money.

9 Ways to Build Trust with Your Lenders

Here are nine specific ways you can build trust with potential lenders:

#1: Get to know your potential lenders

If you're in a professional sales position, what do you do for your clients? You take them to ball games. You take them to lunch—*good* lunch. You might spend $100 on that lunch, including drinks. Is $100 worth it in order to get the sale? You bet it is. Similarly, is it worth it for you to invest $100 in a fancy lunch in order to get a $200,000 loan from someone? Yes! It doesn't even have to be a $100 lunch. You just have to take the time to make an impression. Get to know your potential lenders. Make it about them. Don't sit down and become a talking head. You have to cultivate a real relationship with that person.

#2: It's about what they want—not what you want

The real question is not what they can do for you, but what you can do for them. People want to know how lending money to you is going to help them reach their goals faster.

Three months after investing my brother's money, he sent me a text message that read, *I love getting your checks every month!*

That check going to his mailbox every month was much more valuable to him than getting one payout at the end of the year. You see, my brother's biggest problem was that he needed income—not money. There's a big difference. It doesn't matter how much money you have sitting in the bank if you need income—money you can spend on taking care of your life. That's what it takes to retire.

He was on disability with a bad back. Some days he couldn't get out of bed, and sometimes he was able to get up and play football. His day-to-day life was uncertain. He wanted certainty. I was able to help him reach that goal within days of placing his investment with me. Not months. Not years. Days.

#3: Get to know their money

Where is their money? Is it in an IRA, the stock market, a bank?

What is their current return? If they have $100,000 sitting in a bank, they're probably getting a return of $100 or less a month. That's not a very good return.

What is the money being used for, or what will it be used for? Retirement? College? Other investments?

What's the story of their money? How did they make it? Was it an inheritance? Is it their life's savings?

If you know all these things about their money, you can talk to them about their money. It's like going on a first date where the goal is to get to know the person you're with. It's the same with this money—get to know it, and if you're lucky, you'll get to take it home with you.

#4: Give a personal guarantee

Technically, these lenders are not lending money to you personally. They are lending money to your LLC or your trust or whatever entity you've set up to protect yourself. Legally, you don't personally owe your lenders any money. You don't have to give a personal guarantee. But do it anyway. It won't make the loan go on your personal credit, and it's going to instill a lot of trust into the relationships you have with your lenders.

#5: Give a confession of judgement

If I don't pay my brother back, he can foreclose on my loan. It would take about nine months and cost him a fortune. It would be a nightmare for him. So, when I borrow from people, I give what's called a confession of judgement. This is a written agreement, signed by me, that accepts the liability and amount of damages that was agreed on. Signing this means I can't dispute the lenders' claims against me if I stop paying them as agreed. It circumvents normal court proceedings and avoids the lengthy legal process that would normally be required to resolve the dispute.

When I give a confession of judgment, I agree that if I miss three payments, the house belongs to the lenders and I will pay any costs associated with them acquiring the property. For example, I bought a $150,000 house with my brother's loan. It's a $150,000 property, but I owe my brother $100,000. Do you think he wants me to make my payments? Well, okay, yeah—he doesn't want to lose the monthly income or go through the hassle of acquiring the property. But if it goes that way, then the worst-case scenario for my brother is that he comes out $50,000 ahead on the deal—assuming I never paid him a penny of the money I owed him in the first place. Not bad!

That's what a confession of judgement does for your lenders.

I often joke that there's probably a lot of people out there who want me dead—just so I will stop making the payments on those properties. It's a morbid joke, I know, but I hope it really drills home the value of the confession of judgment.

#6: Have good legal paperwork

Make sure your arrangement is binding and that it serves to protect both parties. I suggest that you have an attorney review at least your first contract to make sure there aren't any holes in it. If you're using the same agreement again on another deal, just change out the names.

#7: Get a promissory note *and* a mortgage

A promissory note and a mortgage are not the same thing. A promissory note is just a promise that so much money will be paid within such and such timeframe. The mortgage, however, is what gives you the power to collect on that promissory note. It's your collateral. Few people realize that when they go in to close on a house, they are signing two sets of documents—one for the promissory note and one for the mortgage. The former is saying, "you're going to pay, and this is when," and the other says, "if you don't, we can take the property."

#8: Close at a title company

Don't close at Starbucks or in your living room. Don't even close at your real estate office, if you have one. Close at a title company for the sake of your lenders. This legitimizes the whole thing in their minds and adds that extra layer of trust and confidence to the deal.

The second deal I did with my brother was a $75,000 loan. I asked him for the money for a real estate deal, and he said he'd stop by the next day. Twenty-four hours later, my doorbell rang and my brother walked in and threw down a $75,000 check onto my table. I laughed and handed it back to him. "Keep it," I said. "We're going to do this right and go to a title company."

Could I have taken that money in a snap? Yes. But I wouldn't do that to my brother. It's not fair to him, it's not fair to anyone. I want to make sure my lenders are taken care of and that their investments are safe with me—no matter what happens.

Ironically, that's exactly why it was so easy for him to put that check into my hands without all the red tape. He already knew he could trust me and that the investment was going to benefit him. I knew better, though, and I treated that second investment as carefully as I did the first.

#9: Be trustworthy

Once you clear up the concerns and you get that money in hand, make good on your word. Be deserving of their trust. Treat their money better than you would your own money.

When I borrow money from someone, that repayment goes to the top of my bill pile. I want you to think this way, too. I don't care if your electricity is about to be turned off. If you've made a promise to someone that you're giving him $500 a month, that payment better come first. You can live in the dark. If you have that mentality, people will see it in you. You will earn their trust.

How to Prepare Your Pitch

When you find the deal you want, it's time to make your pitch. You will do this by giving a brief to your lender. It's just a quick summary of the deal. You can give this brief in person or in writing.

You need to include the purchase price, the repair cost, the ARV, and the rent/income you anticipate the property will yield. If you want to convince someone what the property is worth, show them real comparisons to other like-properties.

You need to state how and when you will pay the lender back. You need to be very clear on this. Will you be making monthly payments? Quarterly payments? Will it be one lump sum at closing? Some people will ask a lender for a loan for a year with the intention of refinancing at the end of that year. Why do this? Just ask for a longer loan to begin with. Refinance after five or ten years. There's no point in putting yourself under that kind of pressure. Just ask. The worst that can happen is that the person says no and you negotiate other terms. If you start by asking for just one year, you likely just left a lot of years on the table. When I asked my brother for the $100,000 loan, I asked him for a ten-year loan. He asked if he could have it back in eight years. Of course, I agreed!

Finally, you need to state your intentions with the property. Are you going to flip it? Are you going to buy it and hold? My intentions are always to buy and hold. I'm not flipping the house to make a buck the next day. I play the long game.

Your Money Mindset

I coach my students at Investor Schooling how to get a "yes" every time. It can be done, and they're doing it. However, I have to warn you that none of this—none of it—is going to work if you don't get your money mindset right first. (For a deeper discussion on this, go back to *Chapter 1: Money Mindset*.)

I want you to think about a penny. In fact, if you have one in your purse or wallet, take it out and look at it. What is it? What's it worth? If you saw a penny on the ground, would you pick it up? When I ask people this, the answer I get the majority of the time is that they would not pick it up. It's just worth one cent—why would they? Well, with 99 more friends, it's a dollar. That's the equivalent of one month of interest on $1,000 if it were sitting in a bank. You just picked up one month's interest on a thousand bucks.

So, what is a penny really?

If you're not willing to pick up a penny—free money right there for the taking—how will you realize that it's possible to get other people to give you money to invest? I teach people to pick up pennies because it's not about the one cent. It's about the money mindset. In my experience, when my students start to understand this and start pocketing those pennies, what happens next is unbelievable. I have videos of some people telling me, three months later, about how money has started to flow through their lives.

The first time I was told I should start valuing pennies enough to pick them up was at T. Harv Ecker's Millionaire Mindset event. I started doing it, and the results completely blew my mind.

You want other people's money? Start picking up the money you find on the floor. That's other people's money that has found its way to you. Open that door, then wait and see how many other doors will open themselves to you, too.

CHAPTER 13

Be Your Own Bank

Dr. Brent Kesler was a chiropractor and chiropractic coach for fourteen years. A very successful one. He'd built up a chain of successful practices in the Kansas City area and rewarded himself by going into debt for some luxuries. He owned a nice home, a condo on the lake, a boat, a wave runner, and an airplane. Sure, he had some bills to pay, but he could afford to pay them. He was living the life.

But the debt sometimes cast a shadow on his life. Afterall, you never know how long the good life will last. You never even know how long life itself will last.

One day, he stumbled across a unique strategy that would increase his cashflow and allow him to get out of debt much faster. At first, it seemed too good to be true. He didn't even bother taking it seriously. Then, two years later, he started hearing from some of his chiropractor colleagues who were applying that strategy, and they were really doing it! They were getting out of debt and increasing their cash flow, and they weren't working any harder or taking any additional risks or losing control of any of their money to do it.

He was ready to give it a try himself. In February 2008, he gathered all his financials together so he could add up everything he owed to third-party creditors. The grand total came to $984,711—almost a million dollars! He didn't despair, though. He fearlessly implemented the strategies I'm going to outline for you in this chapter, and it took him just thirty-nine months to pay off every single one of his debts.

Almost a million dollars completely paid off in just over three years.

Now do I have your attention?

I hope so! Because this whole system is much easier than you can possibly imagine. It only requires you to do one thing differently. Just one thing. As Brent says, it doesn't require you to change what you are currently doing or ever lose control of your money. When you make this change—this *one* change—it can completely transform your financial life.

So, what is the secret?

The secret is to become your own bank.

You will do this by using a specifically engineered whole life insurance policy with a mutual company that pays dividends, designed for high cash value banking. Brent calls this the Infinite Banking Concept.

Whole Life Insurance

Some of you may even be rolling your eyes right now, thinking that this is going to be some kind of sermon on taking care of your kids when you're gone. It's not. This book isn't about your kids being able to spend your money—it's about you being able to spend your money. So, hear me out.

First of all, I need to make a distinction here. I'm specifically talking about purchasing whole life insurance *with a mutual company that pays dividends*. A mutual company, or mutually-owned company, is structured so that the policy holders share in the profits and dividends of the company instead of corporate shareholders. This creates a "co-op" ownership structure that allows profits to funnel to the policyholders as tax-free dividends. That's the kind of setup that's going to give you the best financial returns on your money so that you can do the things you want to do while you're *living*. After all, that's what life is about, right?

With this kind of policy, a portion of each of your premium payments is earmarked for "cash value." It works very much like a Roth IRA in the sense that all of the dollars that go into that cash value account are after-tax dollars, so you won't have to pay any taxes on those dollars or their growth when you take them out later. Unlike a Roth IRA, however, you're not as limited in how much you're able to put into the account in a year's time. Now, there are some limits because you can't overstuff your cash value policy. If you do, the entire policy will be ruined because, at that point, it is no longer be considered a whole life insurance policy contract—it becomes a modified endowment contract (MEC). You'll be subject to different tax laws, which you absolutely do not want.

Your cash value balance continues to grow with each premium payment and all those dollars are set aside to collect uninterrupted compound interest and dividends, all of which are tax-free. Your policy performance has a guaranteed compounding interest growth and has no correlation to the market.

The dividends aren't guaranteed, because those do fluctuate with the market, along with how the company's investment portfolio is doing at the time, but there are companies out there that have had positive returns and doled out dividends for 100-plus consecutive years in a row—companies that were even paying out dividends during the Great Depression. If you're doing business with a company like that, the probability of dividends hitting your account this year and the next are pretty high.

The longer you pay into the policy, the higher the percentage of funds being set aside for that cash value account. All of that money becomes money you can borrow against. Eventually, as your cash value continues to mature and accumulate, you can even draw out some cash—not as a loan, but as a supplement to your income.

Become Your Own Bank

In fact, borrowing against your cash value balance can be even more lucrative than just paying for things in cash. It sounds impossible, but it's true. I'm going to map this out for you, so don't start shaking your head just yet.

Let's say you want to buy a car for $25,000. You happen to have that whole amount currently sitting in your standard savings account at a bank, where it is accumulating 4 percent interest each year. You tell the banker that you want to take out all that money so you can pay for your car in cash, and the banker just laughs. He says, "Tell you what—instead of that, why don't you leave your money here and let me give you a $25,000 loan and charge you 6 percent interest for 60 months?"

You'd probably laugh right back and take your cash and go, wouldn't you?

Well, maybe you shouldn't be so quick to react. You see, in reality, letting the entire $25,000 sit in your bank and grow at an annual rate of 4 percent over the next five years will make you more money than it will cost you in interest on a five-year loan at 6 percent interest. *How can that be, Larry? Four percent gains can never be more than 6 percent losses!*

It's because your loan balance is decreasing every month. That six percent interest will be a smaller and smaller number every single month. The money left in your savings account, however, will always be the exact same amount—$25,000. That 4 percent interest—$1,000 to be exact—is going to keep accumulating on the entire principal every year (and actually go up because of compounding interest). So, one goes up and the other goes down. But our minds are not programmed to think this way. We automatically think that if we earn four and pay six, we are losing two. But that is not how money works. Percentages are all relative. Consider this: Six percent of $25,000 is more than 4 percent of $25,000. However, 6 percent of $1 is not.

I recently borrowed against my policy, and I borrowed at 5 percent. I pay the life insurance company 5 percent, but they give me 4 percent interest. That means it is costing me 1 percent to borrow the money. The only difference is that the insurance company continues to give me interest and I continue to have that cash value at all times. So, I am double dipping on my cash. I am able to leave it inside my policy, forever earning interest, and use it at the same time.

The Myth of Compound Interest

The cool thing about this whole life insurance thing is that you are able to get the compounding interest on stationary money while also keeping that same money in motion. This sounds completely backwards, I know—but it's true.

So, the way that compounding interest works best is for you to leave your money alone for as long as possible. Then, as your principal deposit grows with interest, the overall interest being paid to you continues to go up. For instance, if you have $100,000 sitting in a bank accruing 4 percent interest, then you will have $104,000 sitting in your account at the end of the year. The next year, you will receive interest on $104,000, which will be $4,160, giving you a total balance of $108,160 at the end of year two. The third year, you will receive interest on $108,160, which will be $4326.40, bringing your total balance to $112,486.40 at the end of year three, and so on and so forth.

I love compounding interest! Who doesn't? But the problem is that in order to get the most out of that arrangement, you have to leave as much money in the account as possible for as long as possible, without touching it, or you interrupt the compounding interest.

The thing is, though, that your money isn't staying still at all. As soon as you put your deposit into the bank, it's swept up into a current of exchange. How do banks turn their liability into an asset? They lend it! Banks are in the lending business. Your money is moved around many, many times before you make your next withdrawal. They are leveraging your money to get a return, which they then pocket. The banks are using your money to make a good living for themselves.

A whole life insurance policy with a mutual company that pays dividends allows you to do that yourself, with your own money. You become your own bank.

Stay in Control of Your Money

Let's talk about who is in control of your money. When you borrow money from the conventional bank, you have to pay them back—with interest—and you never give it a second thought because you know that if you don't, the bank will come foreclose on the house or come seize whatever asset you assigned for collateral. Inside my whole life policy designed for banking, I play honest banker with myself and pay myself back and with interest (because if I don't, all I am saying is the banker's money is more valuable than my money and that is simply not true). However, loans on the policy are never required to be paid back; a loan on the policy is simply a pre-payment of the death benefit. At the time of my passing, any outstanding loans will be deducted from my death benefit that will go to my beneficiary. The insurance company is guaranteed to get their loan money returned because I am guaranteed to die! Do you think a regular bank would go for that? No way. As soon as you missed one payment, they'd be sending collection notices or putting a boot on the car.

How the Magic Happens

In order for this strategy to work for you, you need to find someone who is able to help you set up this specifically designed policy for your financial goals—ideally someone who is also actively using this strategy. When you do this, you will get to determine the premium deposit you put into your new "privatized bank"—the privatized bank of *you*.

When you consider that your whole nest egg is able to sit and accrue interest while you're paying back a shrinking loan with an interest rate that is maybe one or two percent higher, this means that you're often able to pay less on your interest payment than you're making on interest. In the worst-case scenario, you just have a line of very, very cheap credit.

A lot of my students are real estate investors who can always use a cheap source of liquidity and financing options. When you go this route, you don't even need to bother with credit applications or paperwork. You don't have to come up with massive amounts of collateral or pledge any of your assets, because your cash value balance already provides those things. You as the policy owner have first access and rights to your cash sitting in the policy.

This, ladies and gentlemen, is the power of becoming your own bank. This is where you can leverage the true value of your whole life insurance policy with a mutual company paying dividends. Instead of borrowing money from a bank and paying that bank interest, you're basically borrowing money from yourself and paying yourself back with interest. You do that by borrowing against the general funds of the insurance company while your full cash bucket in the policy is forever earning you an uninterrupted compounding interest. If you want to buy a car, a house, or put some money toward the things on your bucket list, or whatever you can imagine, you can pull that money out of your policy.

As far as loans go, there's really nothing else like this on the planet.

Find the Right Policy

Before you close this book and run out there to sign up for insurance, you need to understand that not all policies are created equal. You need to work closely with your agent to ensure that you're creating a policy that will specifically be structured for high-cash value. A lot of agents just want to know how much money you want in your death benefit, and then your premiums will be priced accordingly.

This strategy requires the opposite perspective. How much money do you want to pay in? The more you pay in, the more financial leverage you have while you live. Yes, it will buy you a certain amount of death benefit, but that's almost irrelevant to what I'm showing you here.

So, the key questions you need to ask when you're shopping around are as follows:

- How quickly will my policy build cash value and allow me to take out a loan?
- Is this a mutual company that pays dividends?
- How many years in a row has the company paid dividends to its policy holders?
- Does this company use direct or non-direct recognition for its loans?
- Do you have to pay back your loans, or can they just be repaid from your death benefit?
- Is the representative you're considering working with actively applying these strategies—is it someone who is walking the walk?

These are the questions that will help you leverage this strategy the best.

This is What the Super Wealthy Do

Listen, I'm not a life insurance salesman. I'm not going to sit down across the table from you and go into all of the nitty gritty details on your personal financial goals or how much you personally want to invest into your policy. I will leave that to Brent, the chiropractor who now sells these policies full time. If you want to crunch the numbers, call him or look him up at www.themoneymultiplier.com. He'll be happy to help you.

I do, however, want you to understand that having a whole life insurance policy in a mutual company that pays dividends is a real wealth-building tool that sets the foundation for your financial toolbox. The proof is in the fact that this exact strategy is one the super wealthy leverage. They understand that it's not about the death benefit—it's about making your money work for you *now*.

Believe it or not, the number one purchasers of whole life insurance in the world are conventional banks. They own more in whole life insurance than they do in all of their land and their buildings combined. This is called "Bank Owned Life Insurance," or BOLI. They purchase this insurance on their top executives and most valuable employees, but the death benefit is only a part of the reason why. In truth, they understand that holding these policies gives them a tax-shelter for existing funds and a tax-free source of out-going funds.

The premiums paid into a whole life insurance policy have a tax-free cash redemption value. Many banks use this cash to fund their employee benefits plans and other employee premiums *and* cover their employee benefits with the exact same cash—all tax free, no less.

At the same time, the cash value of the insurance policy is growing at a set interest rate each year. Those gains are tax-free. That means that a return of 4 percent per year, tax-free, is the equivalent of a taxable investment gain of 5.5 percent or more. That's a huge return for a bank investment with tax equivalent yields.

Recycle Money into Your Own Pocket

I hope you're starting to see how valuable this strategy can be as a wealth-building tool—especially for investors. All you're going to do is replace the bank with you. You're doing all of these things anyway. You're already buying homes, buying cars, doing remodels, and using credit cards. The only difference is that you're going to recycle all of that money and keep it in the family. This is what the Rockefellers, the Morgans, Stanleys, and Barclays all understood and knew.

I highly, highly recommend that you leverage the magic of this strategy in order to better secure your financial future—and the future of the generations that will come after you. After all, I can guarantee that one of two things is going to happen to you: you will live or you will die. Either way, *somebody* is going to live better tomorrow if you leverage these strategies today.

To find out more about Brent Kessler and The Money Multiplier, you can go to www.TheMoneyMultiplier.com

CHAPTER 14

Lend Out Your Equity

So, we've talked about several incredible strategies you can use to buy properties—but what about those properties that you already own? I often meet people who have properties on which they owe nothing. They owe zero dollars—either because they've paid it off, or they've bought the property in cash. I tell them, "Go get a mortgage and lend that money out to someone!" Sometimes they listen, sometimes they don't. The ones who do come back and thank me.

I'm going to break this down really thoroughly for you so that you can see exactly why this is an opportunity you don't want to pass up. I'm going to do the math to show you what happens when you don't mortgage that property and lend out the money versus what happens when you do.

The Math

Let's say you own a property worth $150,000 that you bought outright with cash. You owe nothing on it, and you're renting it out for $1,500 a month. Your monthly expenses on that property are about $600 a month, which gives you a net cash flow, or Net Operating Income, of $900 a month. When you multiply that out for the year, it comes to an NOI of $10,800. The return on the investment is 7.2 percent. This is called your capitalization rate, or your cap rate, and is the yearly return you receive on your property investment in rent, expressed as a percentage. (To calculate your cap rate, you divide your NOI by the price of your investment property, then multiply by 100 in order to get the percentage of your return.)

So, 7.2 percent—that's not a bad deal—I have no problem with that. But why in the world would you leave $150,000 in this property when you could put it to work somewhere else and get an even higher rate of return?

So, let's say you decide to leverage that property. You go to the bank, and you're approved for a $100,000 mortgage. (It's a rental property, so the bank won't give you everything.) You borrow that money for twenty years at 5 percent interest. Your monthly payment will be $660 a month.

Then what you want to do is take that $100,00 and lend it to someone else for twenty years at 8 percent interest. At first glance, you're probably thinking, *Yay, I'll make 3 percent!* But it's actually so much better than that. It's going to blow your mind.

I'll show you.

Now, the other person's loan payment back to you is going to be $836 a month. So, here's where you're at:

+$900 net cash flow from rent being collected on the property
- $660 loan payment made for your mortgage on the property
+$836 payment back to you on the loan you've extended

+ $1,076 net cash flow on the property

So, you've taken out a loan on a property that was already a source of positive cashflow, and now you've multiplied that cash flow so that it's making you even more money—$176 more, to be exact.

But wait—there's more!

Let's go five years out and assume everything has gone exactly as planned.

In five years, you still owe the bank $83,455. The person you've lent the money to still owes you $87,526. The difference between what you owe and what is owed to you is a positive $4,071. In addition to that, you've been collecting an extra $176 a month for sixty months by now, which has given you an increase of $10,560. So, at this point, you're up $14,631. You earned that extra money by doing nothing.

Now, let's go ten years out.

In ten years, you owe $62,222. The person you've lent the money to still owes you $68,941. The difference is $6,719. In addition to that, you've been collecting an extra $176 a month for 120 months now, which has given you an increase of $21,120. This brings your total increase to $27,839.

Now, we're going to fast forward twenty years—all the way to the end of these loans.

In twenty years, you owe nothing. The person paying you back owes you nothing. However, the difference in what you paid on your loan ($158,400) versus what was paid to you on what you lent out

($200,640) is $42,240. That's how much you netted on that loan in monthly payments over the course of those two decades.

All this because you chose to take my advice and borrow money against the house you bought in cash and lend it to someone else at 8 percent.

So, I promised you I would show you the difference between how much you'd make on this property by following my advice and extending a loan against your mortgage versus not following my advice. You can see that the difference between the two scenarios is a grand total of $42,240—that's the difference in what you will make over that period of time.

But what are the grand totals themselves?

Total Cash Increase *without* extending the loan: $216,000
(144% increase)

Total Cash Increase *with* extending the loan: $258,240
(172% increase)

That's a pretty good return on your investment!

There are some major flaws in these calculations, though.

Remember that $1,500 rent payment you've been collecting? There's no way that's going to stay the same over twenty years. If I adjust that number and raise it by 1.5 percent a year—which is a very small rent increase each year—that's going to give you another $56,226 over that twenty-year period. You also need to factor in the increased property value. If we figure that the property value increases by 5 percent a year, which is the market average, then your property will be worth $379,043 twenty years later. That's an increase of $229,043.

So, the *true* return on your $150,000 investment over twenty years looks like this:

Total Cash Increase *without* extending the loan: $501,269
(334% increase)

Total Cash Increase *with* extending the loan: $543,509
(362% increase)

I hope this has your mind moving. I hope it makes you see every single dollar you have differently. Do you see the potential here?

Rinse and Repeat

Now, let's take this even deeper. This is where things get really interesting.

In year one, you borrowed $100,000 out of a property worth $150,000. In year ten, you will have paid down that loan to $62,222 and your property will now be valued at about $232,700. Couldn't you take out another $100,000 mortgage on that and do it all over again?

Yes. You can. Please do!

Then, do it again in year fifteen when the first loan is close to being paid off and the property is worth $297,000. Then, there's another opportunity in year twenty when the first debt is completely paid off and the house is worth $379,000. You can do this over and over again. Suddenly, that $42,240 increase starts to snowball. By year twenty, assuming you had taken out a second loan in year ten and a third loan in year fifteen, you would have netted a cumulative $84,710 from the three loans ($42,240 from loan one, $27,839 from loan two, and $14,631 from loan three)—bringing your total ROI on that cash property up to $585,979 (391% increase).

All that from one property you bought in cash.

It's important that it's a cash asset because otherwise all of your positive monthly cash flow goes away. However, let's say you have a mortgage on a property but you also have $150,000 of equity in that house. My suggestion is to leverage that equity and go buy a house for $150,000 and do everything else exactly as I've outline here.

It will become the gift that keeps on giving, and you will thank me, too.

CHAPTER 15

How to Choose Stocks

A lot of people don't fully understand what stocks are. They have some idea of how the market works but not enough to leverage that knowledge to their benefit. If you know some—but not enough—this can make you over-confident and lead to you taking risks that will hurt you. Or, you might not take any at all. Both scenarios can be devastating—over-confidence is just as bad as over-caution. One leads to making messes, and the other leads to staying stuck in them.

Now, I'm not here to teach you all about stocks—that would be an entire book unto itself—but I do want you to understand enough about them so that I can dispel some of the big myths you're going to encounter as you continue to educate yourself on how they work. So, we're going to start with the basics and go up from there.

First, we will begin with definitions so that you know what the heck I'm talking about in the next couple chapters. So, don't skip ahead. Reading this chapter will be the difference between knowing what I'm talking about and thinking you know what I'm talking about. Big difference.

What are Stocks?

So, let's first answer this question: What are stocks? It doesn't get much more basic than that. Stocks are literally ownership. When you purchase a company's stock you then own a piece of that company. Each share you have represents another piece you own. This gives you—a common share holder—the right to vote on major issues affecting the company, such as mergers, acquisitions, liquidations of the corporate assets, and more. As an owner, you get a say. Most stockholders, however, own such little pieces of the company that their voices aren't heard. Your voice is as loud as the number of shares you own. When you're talking about millions upon millions of possible shares out there and you maybe own a hundred versus a major corporation, such as a mutual fund, that owns a million shares, you can see how your voice isn't going to be heard as easily. But it's still there. You're still invited to the table to give your vote.

As an owner, you make money in the stock market as you buy and sell your pieces of the company. If you buy shares at $40 per share and then the price per share goes up to $50, you can sell your shares and make a $10 profit per share. The other side of that, though, is that the price per share can also go down and you could end up taking a loss. It doesn't take a huge shift to make the difference, either. Even small market movements can have a big impact on your trading account. This can work against you, leading to large losses, or it can work for you, leading to large gains. It's important to remember that.

As an owner, you may also be entitled to dividend payments as a shareholder of the company. Dividends are portions of the company's profits that are paid out to its shareholders. As an owner, you get a piece of that. It makes sense. If you owned a company outright and that company became profitable, you'd obviously expect to pocket that increase. It's the same thing.

So, what kind of companies do you want to own? There is really only one answer to that question: good ones! That's obvious. What's not so obvious, though, is which companies are the good ones. A lot of people chase the big names when they want to start investing into stocks: Apple, Microsoft, Google, Wells Fargo—all of the names that everyone knows. The problem with that, though, is that "popular companies" are not always synonymous with "profitable companies" in the world of stocks. Microsoft is a great example of this. Its stock fell 37 percent between 2000 and 2013. At the same time, its revenues were going up. The company clearly wasn't failing if its overall revenues were rising.

So, what gives?

Microsoft stocks were simply overvalued in 2000, and adjustments were made to reflect its actual value. (We'll talk more about that phenomenon later.)

So, then—how do you determine which companies are the good ones? The for-real good ones?

There are a lot of factors to consider when answering that question. In order to analyze the security or predict the future of a stock, you have to start with understanding the basics of what makes stock prices go up or down. Even more important, you have to understand how the stock market really works. So, let's begin.

How to Analyze Stocks

Below is a screenshot of Apple computer stocks—ticker symbol AAPL—taken from CNBC.com. (These numbers will be out of date by the time you read this, but that's irrelevant to its usefulness in explaining these principles to you, so just go with me on this.) There are many other websites you can use, and each one will look a little different, but the information they give you will be the same.

The first thing you want to do is look at the top part of the graph, where you see "1D, 5D, 1M," and on and on. These refer to different lengths of time: "1-Day, 5-Day, 1-Month," etc. Depending on what you select, the chart will show you the activity within that period of time. When you first pull up the stock page, it's going to automatically show you the 1-Day chart, which shows you what happened during the day.

The day is measured by the hours the stock market is open, which is 9:30 AM to 4 PM EST on weekdays. These are the trading hours. In this example, when the market closed on that day, the price of AAPL stock was $290.01. However, you will also notice on the page a reference to "extended hours." Only certain traders can trade within those later hours. Most likely, this isn't something that's going to apply to you, but it's still nice to know it's there, and you can see what the extended hours' price would be. In this example, you can see that the stock actually went down by one cent during those extended trading hours after the market closed, which will be reflected in the new stock price when the market reopens the next morning.

Key Stats

Below the graph, you'll see an area labeled "Key Stats." The key stats in a stock are generally considered to be what determine whether the stock is a good stock or not. They give you a pretty good snapshot of how the stock is doing right now and how it's been doing over a long period of time. You'll see today's high price, today's low price, the 10-day average volume of shares being traded, the year-to-date price change as a percentage, and the one-year price change as a percentage.

SUMMARY NEWS PROFILE EARNINGS PEERS FINANCIALS OPTIONS OWNERSHIP

KEY STATS

Open	208.50	52 Week High	233.47	Market Cap	944.6B
Day High	209.32	52 Wk Hi Date	2018-10-03	Shares Out	4.5B
Day Low	206.66	52 Week Low	142.00	Dividend (TTM)	3.08
10D Avg Vol	26.7M	52 Wk Lo Date	2019-01-03	Div Yield (TTM)	1.47%
Beta	1.24	YTD % Chg	32.38	1 Year % Chg	-6.35

RATIOS/PROFITABILITY(TTM)

EPS	11.51	Revenue	259.0B	Gross Margin	37.90%
P/E	18.16	ROE	51.65%	Debt To Equity	112.40%
EBITDA	76,545.00	Net Margin	21.08%		

EVENTS

Earnings Date	2019-10-30	Ex Div Date	2019-08-09	Div Amount	0.77
Split Date	-	Split Factor	-		

First, you'll see the high and low for today. In this example, today's high for this stock was 209.32, and today's low was 206.66. That's a pretty big movement. That's almost a three-point difference.

When you look at the 10-day average volume of shares being traded in this example, it's at 26.7 million shares. This is helpful because sometimes you can look and see today's volume and recognize that today's volume is higher than normal or lower than normal. That is something you want to look at because if it's lower than normal, you want to ask, "What's going on with the stock?" And if it's higher than normal, you will also want to ask, "What's going on with the stock?"

All of these numbers are indicators.

The next numbers you'll look at are the year-to-date change and the one-year change. The year-to-date change in this example shows that this stock went up 32.38 percent compared to where it was on January 1, and the one-year change shows it down 6.35 percent compared to where it was twelve months ago.

Then, you want to look at the "Beta," which is just below the 10-day average. This is an important indicator. It basically tells you how volatile this stock is. The closer it is to 1, the more stable it is. In this example, the Beta number is 1.24, which means it's theoretically 24 percent more volatile than the market. That's not too bad. However, if you were to see a Beta number here of 1.9 or something, then you know that is an extremely volatile stock, and it's going to have some massive mood swings. It is going to fly up and down really fast. That's what they are trying to show you here. There may be other indicators of that as well, but that's what this Beta number is trying to show you at a glance. (However, I wouldn't count so much on Beta as much as support and resistance, which we will talk about in *Chapter 17: Steak and Tuna*.)

Market Cap and Shares Out

The next numbers to look at are the "Market Cap" and "Shares Out." The Market Cap—or market capitalization, as it's really called—shows you the total number of shares the company can give out. In this example, it can sell a maximum of 944.6 billion shares to shareholders. The Shares Out shows you the total amount of shares currently being held by shareholders. In this example, there are 4.5 billion shares out.

These numbers give you a good sense of what the company is worth. If you want to calculate the price of the company, you can take the market cap and multiply it by the current price per share. However, the price of the company is a little different than the *value* of the company.

Twitter and Snapchat are perfect examples of this. At the time of this writing, Snapchat is selling for $75 per share and Twitter is selling for $69 per share. Which is the better value? Well, Twitter's market cap rate is at 55 billion while Snapchat's market cap rate is at 118 billion. At a glance, you might think that means that Snapchat stock is worth twice as much as Twitter stock. No! In fact, my advice would be to buy Twitter stock over Snapchat because these numbers show that Twitter has more room to grow. In my opinion, Snapchat should be selling at more like $35 per share, so buying it now means you'd be paying twice as much as you should be.

Dividends

Next, you'll check out the dividend. A dividend is really simple, as we talked about earlier. It's a portion of the company's profits that is paid out to you as a shareholder. The number there tells you how much. So, according to this example, if you were to put your money in this stock, you would get a dividend of $3.08 per share, which is a dividend yield of 1.47 percent. That's the extra cash that comes back to you per share, just by being an owner of the company.

Some traders invest into the stock market and live off the dividends of their investments. You can do that. However, in this example, I would say that 1.47 percent isn't a very high return on your investment, strictly from an investment's standpoint. The average return in the stock market is about 7 percent. The 1.47 percent here isn't much different than what you'd expect to see by simply putting your money in the bank. Personally, as a real estate investor and options trader, the yields on my investments are much, much higher than that. Even my real estate yields are an average of 10 to 12 percent. So, the number here—the dividends—it's not the greatest thing, but it's a nice, safe place to be.

Earnings Per Share (EPS)

Below all the Key Stats, you'll see the next section labeled "Ratios/Profitability." The first thing you'll see under that is "EPS," or Earnings Per Share. This is an important piece of your analytics of a stock. This number is a reflection of the company's profits divided by the number of outstanding stocks there are. The higher the EPS, the more valuable the company is considered to be.

In short, it's the average profit shareholders make per share. In this example, the EPS is $11.51, which isn't too bad.

EBITDA

A little below that, you'll see the "EBITDA," which stands for Earnings Before Interest, Tax, Depreciation, and Amortization. But honestly, you can pretty much just forget about the words after

"Earnings." Just know it is earnings, which is basically a measurement of the company's performance. Once you know that number, you can compare one company's earnings against the earnings of another company in order to compare stocks. Even then, it's not that important to know, but it's still nice to know when your company is doing well.

Debt to Equity

On the right, you'll see a number called "Debt to Equity." This number tells you how much debt the company has compared to its equity. The higher the number, the more debt the company has. In this example, the Debt to Equity is 112.40 percent, which isn't great.

Gross Margin

The "Gross Margin" of the company basically tells you how much profit the company is making on each transaction it makes. It's the difference between the revenue and the cost of goods sold, divided by the revenue (for you visual folks, the formula looks like this: [revenue-cost of goods sold]/revenue=Gross Margin), with the total number being expressed as a percentage. In our example, the gross margin is 37.9 percent. This tells us that if the company buys something for a dollar, it is basically selling it for $1.38. The company just made 38 cents, or 38 percent, on that transaction. That's a very high number. Car dealers, for instance, have gross margins of about 10 percent. So, this company is doing fairly well. Now, that's the *gross* margin, of course, so it doesn't take out any other costs associated with that transaction, but it still gives you a valuable snapshot of what's going on.

Net Margin

That brings us to the "Net Margin" of the company. The net margin is the percentage of revenue remaining after all the operating expenses, interest, taxes, and preferred stock dividends have been deducted from the company's total revenue. This is the "real" number, if you will. In our example, the net margin is 21.08 percent, which, again, is a very good number. Some successful supermarkets consider a 2 percent net margin to be okay. So, by comparison, this is a very great number and a great stock.

Return on Equity

Next, let's look at the ROE, or "Return on Equity." This is how much profit a company generates with the money shareholders have invested. Looking at our example, we see that this company is taking your money and generating a profit of 51.65 percent. Not bad!

P/E

The P/E, or the "Price Per Earnings," is a very important piece of information you need to know. It is also called "the multiple." This is the ratio of the stock price per share to the earnings per share. Basically, it is how many times the earnings the stock is selling for. For example, let's say you have a small drug store and every year you make a profit of about $100,000. When you decide you want to sell that store to someone else, how do you decide the purchase price? How do you value the company? You're obviously not going to sell it for $100,000, because that's only one year's profit. It's way too low. Typically, for a good small business, you would sell your company for five to six times your annual profit, or your annual "earnings." That means you'd sell your little drug store for half a million dollars to $600,000 and everyone would walk away happy.

In our example, the P/E is showing you that this company is selling for 18.16 times the earnings, which we'll round down to 18 for the purposes of this explanation. So, here, the company is saying, "If we were to sell the entire company of Apple to somebody, we would sell it at this current stock price, which would be 18 times the earnings, meaning 18 times what the company is making per year." It's a little high, but not horribly high, and certainly not too high. Not for Apple.

Now you can see where the stock price of $209, in our example, is coming from. You take the earnings per share and multiply by the price per earnings to get 209. For this reason, P/E is also referred to as "the multiple." When you hear the phrase "What multiple is such and such stock selling at," they're talking about the P/E.

This is an important piece of information when you're comparing stocks. If you are looking at two companies and you see that one has a big multiple and the other has a small multiple, the one with the smaller multiple is more likely to be a stock that is either very secure or it is more likely to go up, where a higher multiple has a higher likelihood of going down. The reason for this is because if the multiple is already very high, there isn't much room for it to go up from there—whereas if it's low, there's plenty of room to grow.

What is a Good Multiple?

So, what is a good multiple? It comes down to how much above the company's value the consumer is willing to pay. But all of that is a little bit arbitrary, really. For instance, let's look at some of the multiples of commonly held companies.

In our example, at the same time that Apple has a multiple of 18, Ford has a multiple of 6.04, meaning Ford is selling for six times its earnings. I consider that to be pretty low—especially for a company like Ford—but it's a decent number overall.

When we look at IBM, we see it has a multiple of 13.53.

Another popular company is Disney. In this example, Disney's multiple is 18.22. Again, that's not a terribly high multiple, but it's about the same as Apple. So, those two companies are valued about the same.

Okay, so now we are starting to build a spectrum of multiples across these companies. We are starting to get an idea of what a "normal multiple" looks like.

But now let's look at another one. Let's look at Facebook.

In this example, Facebook is trading at a multiple of 44.35. Wow! If you compare that to Apple's 18, you're probably thinking, *How is that possible*? Well, this is how multiples sometimes get out of hand. What analysts are saying with this number is that they believe Facebook has so much growth potential that it's worth paying almost 45 times the earnings because they know that, very shortly, it is going to be making 45 times the earnings and the price of the stock is going to go up and the multiple will go down. They believe it's that good. (It's true that as the stock price goes up, and if the earnings per share stay the same, then the multiple goes down.)

It may sound outrageous, but I have to be honest with you—I agree. I think Facebook is that good. I think Facebook is going to take over the world.

Let's move on to another head-scratcher. In this example, Amazon's multiple is 171.81. That's unbelievable! You may think, *How can anyone think that Amazon is worth 172 times its earnings*? It does seem kind of bizarre when you look at numbers like this. It can be hard to make sense of it.

Just wait until you see Netflix.

In this example, Netflix is trading at a multiple of 333. If you think that is absolutely insane, I agree with you. To me, this stock is worth a fraction of that. I would value it at a multiple of about 10 to 30. It is unbelievable to me that this multiple is so high. I see that number and automatically think they are going to have a "Microsoft situation" and the market will soon likely make adjustments to this number so that it reflects its actual value. (As of the writing of this book, it is actually down to 58.59.)

So, now that we're seeing this growing spectrum of multiples, I want you to take a second and ask yourself what you think Google will be trading at. I mean, it's *Google*. After seeing the numbers for Amazon, Facebook, and Netflix, come up with a guess for Google. What are you thinking? Five hundred? Seven hundred? A thousand?

Check this out: In this example, Google is trading at a multiple of 28.99.

Huh?!

Now you can see where multiples can get very confusing. But remember, as the stock prices go up, and if the earnings per share stay the same, then the multiple goes down. It's at 28.99 *now*, but it was many times that number back in the day as it was positioning itself to be the empire it is today. (Whoever made that bet became a wealthy man, I can tell you that.)

Clearly the multiple is a bit arbitrary. If it wasn't, you could just bet against Netflix all day long and say Netflix *has* to come down. It's not that simple, though. When you look at the three- to four-month history of Netflix in this example, you can see that Netflix just keeps going up.

So, what is it, then? What is the secret to safely placing your bets in the stock market?

Well, now you have an idea of what all these numbers mean when you're looking at and comparing stocks, but now you're also starting to realize that this is just the beginning of understanding.

But before we move into the next chapter and add another layer to these principles, I challenge you to take some time to practice drilling in your understanding of *this* chapter. So, I'm going to give you some homework: Go check out some of your favorite companies and get fluent in their numbers. What are their stock prices? What are their market caps? What do their dividends look like? What are the multiples of those companies? I guarantee you will find this exercise interesting and that you will likely come across some surprises. Stocks you assumed would be good bets might be stagnant, and vice versa. Do this exercise day after day. You'll see lots of interesting changes. Stock prices change daily, and each change tells a different story.

It's like following a soap opera.

I love it.

CHAPTER 16

Stocks: The Big Picture

In the last chapter, I told you about the indicators you want to pay attention to when it comes to determining how well an individual stock is doing. However, you also need to keep your eye on the stock market as a whole. Specifically, you want to keep track of the DJIA, the S&P 500, the NASDAQ, the Russell 2000, and the VIX.

But before I explain what those are, I need to give you a little more background about the stock market itself in order to put them into context.

Again, the stock market is simply the market in which shares of publicly held companies are issued and traded, either through exchanges or over-the-counter markets. So, let's talk about where these exchanges take place and why they are important.

Official Exchanges

There are many different exchanges where you can buy stocks. Each of these exchanges are like separate department stores. Just as Lowe's and Home Depot sell one kind of product and Kohl's and Sears sell another, these different exchanges specialize in selling and trading in certain niches. The stocks sold in these exchanges are specific to that exchange—they are not sold anywhere else.

You've likely heard of the NASDAQ, even if you weren't really sure what it was. It stands for National Association of Securities, Dealers, and Automated Quotations. But who cares what it stands for? All you really need to know about the NASDAQ is that it usually trades tech stocks. When you hear or see phrases such as "the NASDAQ hit 5,000 today," that number is the NASDAQ composite index, which was created at its inception. People use that number as a gauge of how tech stocks—or NASDAQ traded stocks—are doing.

Then there's the New York Stock Exchange—another "department store." This used to be called the AMEX, or American Stock Exchange. There are other exchanges, too, such as the Tokyo Stock Exchange, London Stock Exchange, Shanghai Stock Exchange, and many others.

Over-the-Counter Stock Exchanges

There is also something else called "over-the-counter stocks." Basically, over-the-counter stocks are not sold in markets. They are basically sold directly between two parties without the supervision of an exchange. Sometimes they are called "pink slips." A pink slip is when you want to buy a company's stock but the company is so small it can't afford to be traded on an exchange (it costs a lot of money to be listed on an exchange). So, you essentially go directly to the company and hand it a buck and it hands you back a pink slip that says you bought so many shares of its stock.

Typically, anything that is selling for under $5 is going to be an over-the-counter stock. You can find some that are as little as a quarter.

Sometimes, you will hear about stocks getting thrown off exchanges. That usually happens when a company's stock gets so low that the exchange it's listed with doesn't want the liability of holding it. In that case, that stock then becomes an over-the-counter stock.

CBOE

There is another thing called the "Chicago Board of Options Exchange," or CBOE. This is very important to me because I trade options. But honestly, you don't really need to know where your options are traded—on the board or not. Ultimately, the most important thing you need to know about options is that there is always a buyer and there is always a seller. Don't worry about who ends up with what from where. Don't worry about if the person who ends up with it is making or losing money. You only have to worry about whether you make or lose money. The neat thing about the Board, though, is that *you* don't need to find the buyers and sellers. It serves as the middleman and makes the magic happen.

How is the Stock Market Doing?

Now that you kind of have an idea of where the stocks reside and how they are organized, let's talk about those larger indicators that tell you how the stock market is doing as a whole.

DJIA

The Dow Jones Industrial Average—the DJIA—was created by a Wall Street journalist. It reports the average of 30 popular stocks.

For instance, when the stock market is up, you might hear something such as "the DOW is up 200 points today." This means that the average increase across those 30 stocks is 200 that day. But it's an average, which means that some of those stocks in the DOW might have gone down, but most of them went up.

The list of companies it is averaging changes from time to time, but you can find out what that list is at any given time really easily. Just type it into Google, and it will come right up. The average is calculated using some crazy formula that adjusts for splits and dividends. Do I know what the formula is? No. Do I care? No. You don't need to know, either. You just need to know that when the DJIA is up, it means the stock market is doing great; when it's down, it's not. Simple as that.

The numbers during the Great Depression really prove my point. In July 1929, the DJIA hit almost $350. In December 1932, it was down to about $60. If that isn't an accurate reflection of how the stock market was doing at the time, I don't know what is.

S&P 500

The next one is the S&P 500. This is basically made up of 500 large-cap stocks (i.e., very big companies) picked from both the NASDAQ and the New York Stock Exchange. The S&P 500 takes the average of those companies. When the S&P 500 is up, things are really good; when it is down, things are really bad. Most of the time, you will see the NASDAQ numbers follow the same trends as the S&P500.

Russell 2000

By now, I bet you can guess how many stocks the Russell 2000 is averaging. You guessed it—2000. However, whereas the S&P 500 is looking at big-cap stocks, the Russell 2000 is looking at small-cap stocks. So, these are smaller companies, which is where a lot of mutual funds put their investments. Because of that, the Russell 2000 is a good indicator of how well mutual funds are doing that day or month.

VIX

The VIX is a particularly important piece of information for a stock options trader. The VIX is a ticker symbol for the Chicago Board of Options volatility index. People call it the fear index or the fear gauge. When the VIX starts hitting 25 and above, the stocks start to get more volatile. It serves a similar purpose at the BETA, which we talked about in the last chapter. If the VIX reaches 35, 40, you know there are some major things about to happen in the stock market. That is a bad time to get in because you are likely going to see crazy movements up and down.

Your Assignment

Now I want you to go and put this information to the test. Did you do your homework from the last chapter and start looking up some of your favorite stocks to see what they're doing each day? I hope you're still following them. Or, if you haven't had a chance to do it yet, that you *will* follow them for a while. But I don't just want you to look at how your individual stocks are doing. Now I want you to compare how they're doing to the market in general. Do you see the correlation? When the Dow is up, what happens to your stocks? Do they go up or down? How about the NASDAQ? What's the correlation there? And so on and so forth. See how these different indicators affect the stocks you are following.

Now you're starting to get an idea of how the stock market really works. But these facts and figures do not touch the most important question of all:

What makes stocks go up or down?

I will answer that question in the next chapter.

CHAPTER 17
Steak and Tuna

Now I've told you the key stats and the indicators you need to keep tabs on in order to track the health of the stock market and your individual stocks. But what makes these numbers go up and down at all?

Ahh, now that is a good question. And the answer is that it all comes down to greed and fear—which is more formally referred to as support and resistance. When you understand and lead with this, you will make fewer mistakes and take fewer gambles.

You see, here is the dark reality you need to know about stocks: There is a backdrop of big money managers working on Wall Street every day who want to take their wives out for steak dinners at the end of the week. These are industrial fund managers working for companies such as Fidelity and Charles Schwab, who manage the purchases and sales of stocks within mutual funds, hedge funds, etc. These fund managers get paid to make money in these transactions so that the funds are profitable, and they get bonuses based on performance. So, if they sell their stocks at the top—or near the top—they're taking their wives out for steak. If not, they're feeding their ladies tuna fish sandwiches.

So, here's what happens:

When a stock goes up, those fund managers are afraid, thinking, *I might be in too high*, or *I'm not going to buy anymore because it's too expensive now—I missed it.* So, they stop buying that stock and suddenly the stock price stagnates and then falls. But then, when the stock goes down, those fund managers get greedy. They decide they're going to buy that stock like crazy because they want to make their bonuses. Hence, the stocks go back up again. It's Supply and Demand 101.

And that's it—that's how the stock market is being ruled by steak and tuna fish.

It's really about fear and greed. To call them by their other names, fear is known as "resistance," and greed is known as "support." These two variables create small movements in the stock market every day. (Small movements are the option trader's money-making opportunity, by the way.) However, those small movements can add up over time and create very, very big movements. I can give you two perfect examples of this: The Great Depression (1929-1939) and The Great Recession (2007-2008).

Below are some other variables that can affect stock prices, but even these are ruled by support and resistance. Allow me to explain:

Earnings Reports

First, let's talk about Earnings Reports. Earnings are reported quarterly and announced as an Earnings Report the month after the ending quarter. For instance, the last quarter ends December 31st, so the Earnings Report comes out some time in January or early February. This gives the company time to prepare the audit, or whatever they have to do for accounting purposes, and also gives the company time to prepare a statement (either for damage control or for *congratulations!*—depending on whether the earnings were good or bad) for their shareholders. So, it takes them about a month to create the Earnings Report.

These reports provide investors with three things: an overview of sales, expenses, and net income for the last three months. They will likely also give a comparison to last year's numbers and possibly to the previous quarter as well. If the report shows the company hasn't done well, the stock typically goes down; if the report shows the company has done well, the stock typically goes up. But not always. In fact, one of my biggest losses was the result of betting on earnings because I knew this stock was going to do really well—and it did—but there was something said in the report that made everybody panic, and then the price of that stock plummeted.

You might find a stock that you think is going to do really well, and you might reasonably want to bet on the earnings by buying the stock or the options right before that report comes out. You anticipate there's going to be a spike in the stock price, and you want in on that. Well, that sounds great—it really does—but I promise you this strategy is purely a gamble. That's especially true if you're investing into stock options that are scheduled to expire shortly after that report comes out.

I generally admonish all of my students at Investor Schooling to never bet on earnings. There are also times, however, that I tell them to break that rule—but it has to be a careful calculation in which they are simultaneously following a bunch of other rules, too. There are just so many variables that can make the stock price move immediately following the release of that report. The one thing these variables have in common is that they are completely out of your control.

News Articles

One of these variables is news articles. Bad publicity can cause stocks to drop or rise quickly. And there is nothing you can do about it. You don't know when articles are coming, and you don't know what they're going to say.

Unfortunately, these articles are sometimes manipulative—released with the intent to sabotage the system. Remember those fund managers who are hungry for some steak I talked about at the beginning of this chapter? Well, let's say a fund manager is holding stock options that are betting that a certain stock is going to go down. He then writes a bad article about the company to create some panic in the other stockholders, who then start to sell off their stocks, which makes the price per share go down. Just like that, the fund manager created his own self-fulfilling prophecy. And it's perfectly legal! All he has to do is mention in the article that he owns some shares of that stock and he's magically immune to any legal repercussions.

So, beware.

Rumors

Rumors are often spread for these same reasons. "Did you hear that this company is going to buy that company?" When you start reading news articles and following Earnings Reports, you are going to hear those kinds of rumors all the time. The reality, however, is that most rumors are being spread by those same fund managers. Do they make them up? Not always. But they're sure the first in line to pass them on and try to use them to start a buying or selling frenzy. Sometimes it's only for the purpose of manipulation—they don't want to have to stop and get some cans of tuna on the way home. Sometimes their intentions are sincerely to inform. Either way, the reality is that by the time we hear it, it is too late. Forget it. The damage has been done or the money has been made. We, the common shareholders, are the last in line of a long stretch of people playing the telephone game.

My advice, though, is to avoid playing into the game. Don't bet on the rumors because you just don't know what's going to happen. Sometimes the rumor is true, and sometimes the rumor is false. The stock is going down either way. If the rumor is false, the stock is likely going to drop pretty far because it's going to be something shocking and unanticipated. If the rumor is true, however, the stock is likely to go down just a little bit because people have already seen it coming and anticipated that particular development. But again, by the time we hear about it, it is too late.

Play the Long Game

Whatever the variables are at play, they all come back to greed and fear—support and resistance. It is the same thing over and over again. This is why you should consider your stock portfolio a long-term investment, and sometimes a *very* long-term investment.

For instance, if you were to look at a 20-year snapshot of Microsoft's stock, you would see that in 2007, it was at $30 per share. You would also see that it was at $30 per share in 2013. Sounds pretty stable, right? Well, those years in between weren't so good. There was a big dip in 2008. If you'd sold then, you would have taken a massive loss. That was the 2008 crash. But if you take that dip out, the stock stayed relatively the same price for five years. It didn't make any moves until 2013, and then it doubled between 2013 and 2017. If you'd put your money into Microsoft in 2007 and then sat on it through the fear and greed of 2008, holding it until 2017, you would have doubled your money.

It's amazing what that long-term investment strategy can do for you.

CHAPTER 18

Don't Pay Taxes!

My political stance is simple: Show me the new tax, show me the new tax loophole. This has been my political stance for a very long time.

The interesting part about this, though, is that I didn't know I didn't actually understand the tax loopholes until I discovered I didn't. For many years, I operated under the assumption I knew what I needed to know. But several years ago, I was in for a big surprise. My accountant looked me in the eyes and told me what I owed in taxes. I listened to the number, and I smiled and said, "You mean that's my taxable income, right? That's what I'm paying taxes *on*." He shook his head and repeated himself. "No, Mr. Steinhouse. That is what you owe." I waited for him to tell me he was kidding. He waited for me to let it sink it.

The number was so big I almost fainted. I mean, it was big. It was more than what most people make in a year.

That was the moment when I discovered I did not know enough about the tax loopholes. I became a man on a mission. I never wanted to pay so much in taxes ever again—and I certainly didn't want to be surprised by them!

The Rich Pay Less Taxes

I want to teach you how the rich pay less taxes so that you can do it, too. Do you remember when Mitt Romney was running for president? Everyone made a big deal about his tax returns. When they went public, people went crazy because they showed he only paid a 14 percent effective tax rate (I want you to remember that number—14 percent). "How did that rich SOB get away with that?" they wanted to know. "D***, I am paying 32 percent, and I make a fraction of his income!"

I regularly have arguments with people who claim that they pay a higher tax rate than Trump does. First of all, that's the dumbest thing I have ever heard. Second of all, they don't understand the way that taxes are actually calculated.

How Taxes are Calculated

Now, let's talk a little bit about how taxes are calculated. I want to talk about this because I can almost guarantee you that you don't know how your taxes are calculated—and you need to.

First of all, I want you to look at the chart on the next page to determine which tax bracket you're in:

Let's say your adjusted gross income is $100,000 and you are married. This would put you in the 22 percent tax bracket. So, what

Rate	For Single Individuals	For Married Individuals Filing Joint Returns	For Heads of Households
10%	Up to $9,875	Up to $19,750	Up to $14,100
12%	$9,876 to $40,125	$19,751 to $80,250	$14,101 to $53,700
22%	$40,126 to $85,525	$80,251 to $171,050	$53,701 to $85,500
24%	$85,526 to $163,300	$171,051 to $326,600	$85,501 to $163,300
32%	$163,301 to $207,350	$326,601 to $414,700	$163,301 to $207,350
35%	$207,351 to $518,400	$414,701 to $622,050	$207,351 to $518,400
37%	$518,401 or more	$622,051 or more	$518,401 or more

Source: Internal Revenue Service

will your taxes be? At first glance, you're likely to assume it's going to be 22 percent—$22,000—but that would be wrong.

This is how it actually works:

Your first $19,750 is taxed at 10 percent.

The next $60,500 is taxed at 12 percent.

The remaining balance (in this example, $19,750) is taxed at 22 percent.

$19,750 x .1 = $1,975
$60,500 x .12 = $7,260
$19,750 x .22 = $4,345

Total Tax Due = $13,580
Actual percentage of taxes: 13.6 percent

When you do the math here, you'll see that your effective tax rate is 13.6 percent! You're not paying anything close to 22 percent. So, why are people complaining about Mitt Romney paying 14 percent? Not only that, but a lot of folks talk about wanting a 15 percent flat tax. That sounds nice if you don't understand how your taxes are calculated—but if you do, then you realize that the flat tax would actually increase the taxes you owe if you fall within a certain tax bracket. Now, if you're making well over $400,000 a year, yeah—that flat tax is going to save you some money, but you're playing in a completely different ballpark than most Americans.

Deferring Taxes

Now I want to tell you how you can decrease your tax liabilities and pay even less in taxes. Let's talk a little bit about deferring taxes. This is one of my favorite tax loopholes because I don't really want to write checks to the government.

I am going to teach you about several different vehicles you can use to defer your taxes and/or reduce your tax liabilities. I'm going to go so far into this in these next few chapters that when I'm done, you will know how you to legally buy your children's clothes, their cars, and their college educations with pre-tax dollars.

IRAs

IRAs, or Individual Retirement Accounts, are one of the best tools for protecting your income against taxation. There are a few different kinds of IRAs you can put your money into, and we're going to talk about some of the important differences between them. In the following two chapters, we will dive really deep into the benefits and uses of these different IRA options.

Traditional IRA

As of 2021, the traditional IRA allows you to make a personal contribution of up to $6,000 a year ($7,000 a year if you're over the age of 50). Those amounts are subject to change from year to year, but right now, those are the numbers. This is a tax-deferred account, meaning you won't have to pay taxes on that $6,000 right now. You won't pay any taxes on that income and its interest/growth until you take it out later. "Later" is defined as being at least age 59 and a half. If you take it out before then, you will have to pay taxes *and* penalties on your money.

So, that money is not taxed in the year that you invest it into your IRA. It's money you can actually write off on your tax return. I want to illustrate to you exactly what that means, so let's go back to our example above. You will deduct the $6,000 IRA payment (or $7,000 if you are over the age of 50) from the lump of money being taxed at 22 percent:

$19,750 x .1 = $1,975
$60,500 x .12 = $7,260
$13,750* x .22 = $3,025

Total Tax Due = $12,260

Actual percentage of taxes: 12.3 percent

*$19,750 - $6,000 IRA contribution = $13,750

You just saved $1,320 in taxes for that year. That is dollar-for-dollar money that you did not have to pay out to the government.

But remember—in our example, you're married. So, what if you both contribute to an IRA that year? You can deduct another $6,000 from your taxable income! Let's look at that:

$19,750 x .1 = $1,975
$60,500 x .12 = $7,260
$7,750* x .22 = $1,705

Total Tax Due = $10,940

Actual percentage of taxes: 10.9 percent

*$19,750 - $12,000 IRA contributions = $7,750

If you both pay into an IRA, you will reduce your tax payment by $2,640.

Now, it's important to understand, though, that this is tax deferred money—it's not tax free. You will be taxed when you take out the money. If you withdraw those funds early—before you are 59.5 years old—you will be charged a 10 percent penalty on top of the taxes. For example, if you were taking out $10,000 early, you would lose $1,000 in penalties right off the top, in addition to the taxes you will have to pay on that ten grand.

Roth IRAs

Roth IRAs are a little bit different. The amounts you can contribute are the same, but they are after-tax dollars. There's no tax deduction up front. The $6,000 or $7,000 you put in (depending on your age) isn't going to give you a write off that year. You cannot deduct that money from your taxes.

Now, I know you're probably thinking, *Larry, it's not tax free. I had to pay taxes on it before I put it in my Roth IRA!* True, but you don't have to pay taxes on its growth. This is extremely important to understand, and we will really get into the weeds on that in the next chapter.

You see, that $6,000 year after year starts to add up pretty quickly, and hopefully it's being put into some good investments that will bring you a high return. All of that money accumulates in your Roth IRA account, where it is gathering compound interest—more and more the longer it sits. It doesn't matter how much your initial investment grows—you will never have to pay a single dollar of taxes on that growth.

It's the idea of paying taxes on the seeds instead of the crops. It's common sense. If you're in a tax bracket that requires you to give 30 percent of your income to the government, which is going to be less: paying taxes on $6,000 or $6,000+interest? That's not rocket science. I mean, a $20,000 investment could potentially turn into a $1 million deal. Personally, I'd much rather pay taxes on the $20,000!

You might be thinking, *Well, that sounds nice, but what about all those tax deductions I could have received? Those tax deductions for those 20 years were valued at $53,100. I could have saved $13,307!*

Big deal, you saved $13,307 over 20 years. If you're doing this right, you will make a lot more than that on the returns of your Roth IRA investments. We will talk more about that in the next chapter.

SEP IRAs

Now let's talk about retirement plans for your business. That's right—your business. The first thing I want to talk about is a simplified retirement plan—an SEP. This is an IRA, too. And yet, it is so unlike an IRA. You see, you can contribute up to $58,000 to your SEP. Yes, you read that right. There is not an extra zero in there as a typo. You can contribute up to $58,000—not $6,000 or $7,000. It's $58,000 or 25 percent of your income, whichever one is less.

It's great for the small business owner because it has a low cost to create and manage. It is not like a 401k, which businesses have to pay thousands of dollars into.

SIMPLE IRA

The SIMPLE IRA is for business owners and stands for Savings Incentive Match PLan for Employees. It's a little bit different from the SEP IRA. The amount you, as an employee, can contribute to this account will change from year to year. At the time of this writing, you can contribute up to $13,500 of your pre-tax income. If you're 50 or older, you can contribute up to $16,500. Your employer can also contribute to this retirement at up to a 3 percent match.

Some of the advantages of this kind of plan are that you can invest more money into it than you can with the more standard IRA plans and that it's not capped at a percentage of your income. However, the downside is that, if you're an employer, you can't offer any other retirement plan in addition to this one. If you're an employee, however, you can still maintain other retirement accounts. You would, however, be subject to a cap in relation to your 401k. So, if you have a 401k somewhere else and the contribution cap is $19,500 for the year, that money is going to be cumulative across the SIMPLE IRA and the 401k. If you contribute $10,000 to the 401k, you can only contribute up to another $9,500 into the SIMPLE retirement account—not counting anything your employer contributes as a match.

You can pull your money out of this account without a penalty at the age of 72. If you pull it out within two years of putting it in, there is a penalty of 25 percent, which is substantially higher than the 10 percent associated with other types of retirement plans. After the first two years, however, it drops down to a 10 percent penalty.

401k

A 401k retirement account is only available through a for-profit employer. So, if you're self-employed or if you own your own business, you will need to look elsewhere for putting your money away for retirement, such as the SIMPLE or SEP IRAs.

So, here's how the 401k works:

Like the IRA accounts, there are both traditional (pre-tax) and Roth (post-tax) options. These are both investment accounts, which will hopefully grow your contributions over time. However, like all investments, there is some risk involved. It is possible that the investments will go down in value. But don't worry too much—those who manage these kinds of accounts are very strategic in the investments they choose in order to minimize these risks.

The amount you can invest into your 401k will change from year to year. At the time of this writing, you can contribute up to $19,500 a year, which doesn't include anything your employer will contribute. Many employers will match your contributions up to a certain percentage of your income. Take full advantage of this! It's literally free money. It's a match, though, so that money doesn't come automatically. In order to get the money, you have to give some money. For instance, if your employer matches up to 5 percent of your income but you only contribute 2 percent of your income—the employer's contribution will also only be 2 percent.

One drawback of the 401k compared to an IRA is that you don't have a lot of control over where your money is being invested. You are limited to the investment options your employer gives you. So, one strategy for maximizing your retirement options is to invest into your 401k until you've maxed out your employer's match, then contribute to an IRA, and then once you hit the $6,500 cap on your IRA, return to contributing to your 401k.

Also, you can't cash out your 401k before you're 59.5 years old unless you meet the requirements of a hardship exemption, such as extensive medical bills or financial need. In that event, you can pull money out of your account, but you will have to pay a 10 percent penalty, and it will also be counted as income, so you will have to pay income taxes on the money you pull out.

If you change jobs, or if you just want more control over your investments, you can also roll your 401k over to an IRA account. You can roll the entire lump sum over at once—it will not count toward your annual contributions.

Moving 401k to IRA

If you have money in your 401k that you want to move over to an IRA, you can do that, but only once you no longer work for that employer anymore. If you're moving it from your 401k to a traditional IRA, you don't have to pay any taxes on the money being moved and it doesn't count against your cap for that year. However, in almost every scenario, you will have to pay taxes on that money if you're moving it over to a Roth IRA. And of course, now I'm going to tell you about the loophole:

If you put it into a traditional IRA, you do not pay the taxes. That's because you are moving it from a tax-sheltered place to another tax-sheltered place. You can do that all day long. It's just another vehicle.

Then why do you bother moving it over at all? Where's the benefit? Well, you will have moved your money from a 401k that you have no control over into a vehicle that you now have control over. This is especially true if you move it over to a self-directed IRA, which we will talk about in the next chapter.

You see, while you are at the company, your 401k money is trapped. It can only go to where your employer says it can go. You pick your four funds from a short list, and then those are the only funds your investment is going into. Period.

Depending on the actual details of those transactions, sometimes it may be better to leave your tax-deferred money where it's sitting. But generally, as long as you can either pay those taxes without having to take it out of your principal balance or transfer it over and let it sit for at least ten years, it's a good idea to move whatever you can over into your Roth IRA.

The Benefits of Roth IRAs

Why do I recommend the Roth IRA? Well, as I said, I plan on being much wealthier as an old man than I am right now in my prime. So, of course I love the structure of the Roth IRA. Here are a few more reasons why I think they're the best option:

- **No penalties for early withdrawals**: Once you put your money into a traditional IRA, you better have plans of letting it sit until you're at least 59.5 years old because there will be major financial penalties if you pull it out before then. That's not the case for Roth IRAs. You can take out your contributions at any time with zero penalties. Anything you take out above your original contributions, though, would be hit with a 10 percent penalty tax, in addition to the normal taxes. So, let's say you've accumulated $60,000 in contributions and those contributions have grown to $75,000 with interest and dividends. Then, you have some medical emergencies come up and you have to pull that money out to cover your hospital expenses. You can pull out up to $60,000—the amount of your direct contributions—before there are any penalties and fees. If you pull out more than that, you are dipping into the growth and you will be penalized. However, you will only have to pay penalties on the difference. So, if you take out $65,000—$5,000 more than your original contribution—you'd only have to pay fees and penalties on that five grand.

- **No compulsory minimum distributions:** With a traditional IRA, you are required to start taking money out of your account once you turn 70 and a half and every year thereafter. These are called "minimum distributions." You can take more than the minimum, but you can't take less. You may want to anyway—in which case, you won't care—but what if you don't? You may not need the cash and would prefer to keep it in your account where it will continue to grow and work for you. You may not ever need that income again, in which case you'd like to keep it as an asset that is growing and maturing for your posterity or whomever is going to inherit your wealth.
- **No age limit:** With traditional IRAs, you can only contribute until you reach 70 and a half. That's not the case with the Roth IRA, where you can contribute as long as you want to.

- **There's no way to know how much you'll be required to pay in taxes in the future:** The tax codes are always changing. The same amount of income that puts you in the 30 percent bracket right now could put you in a 50 percent tax bracket thirty years from now. We just have no way of knowing. There are a lot of factors that contribute to those numbers—and you have zero control over any of them. Personally, I'd rather pay taxes on my earnings right now, while I have full disclosure on what I'm paying and why. Anything else feels a little too much like Russian Roulette to me.

The Backdoor Roth IRA

One potential snag with the Roth option, however, is that there are income requirements in order to be able to contribute. As of 2021, if your tax filing status is "single" or "head of household," the cap is set at $122,000. If you're filing jointly with a spouse, the cap is $193,000. You have to make less than those numbers in order to qualify to make contributions to a Roth IRA.

Sort of.

You see, there's also this thing called a "Backdoor Roth IRA." It's a strategy that allows you to get around the income cap. What you do is first contribute to a traditional IRA, which has no income limit (there are income limits to how much of your contribution would be tax deductible, though, but we won't go into all of that here). Then, you can transfer that contribution over to a Roth IRA at any time. The catch, though, is that you would have to pay taxes on that money once you transfer it over. That's true for anything you roll over into your Roth IRA that you haven't already paid taxes on, such as your 401k.

However, what if you haven't actually deducted that money from your income yet? You only do that at the end of the year—taxes aren't due until April 15. If you haven't paid those taxes yet—if you haven't literally made that tax deduction from your income yet—you do not have to pay taxes on that $6,000 when you move it over.

I told my accountant I was doing this. I said, "Is there anything else I need to know for this work?"

He asked, "Did you put the money in yet? Because listen, you need to make sure that that money is still at exactly $6,000 when you move it over."

"What do you mean?"

He said, "I know how you trade stock options, and in one day you could turn that $6,000 into $10,000 or $15,000 or $20,000. You don't want that to happen before you have a chance to move it over to the Roth IRA because then you would have to pay taxes on the whole thing."

I moved it over to the Roth IRA immediately.

And that, folks, is the strategy for the backdoor IRA.

Forget about the rules.

Just know the loopholes.

CHAPTER 19

How to Buy Houses with Your IRA

Once you contribute your money into an IRA, your work is far from finished. You see, an IRA, by definition, is not an investment account. It's just a place to put your money away for retirement. If you open your IRA with a bank, it's going to sit there as cash and do very little in the way of growth. You may get a little bit of return, but it's not going to exceed the small percentages the bank offers in its savings accounts, money market, and CDs. You'll get less than a 1 percent return on your money that way. A total waste.

The best way to get the most out of your IRA is to put it somewhere that it will grow. For instance, you can open an IRA with a Mutual Fund company and have all those thousands and thousands of dollars leveraged in various investments. There aren't a lot of limits on where your money can go. That money can be invested into the stock market, mutual funds, notes, ETFs, precious metals, annuities, and more. In some circumstances, you can even invest in real estate, which is one of the things that most excites me personally.

Basically, the only two things that are off limits are collectibles and life insurance (for the full list, check the IRS website). Other than that, you can build out your IRA portfolio the same way you would any other investment portfolio. The difference is that all of your growth from those investments are either going to be tax-deferred, if they're in a traditional IRA; or tax-free, if they're in a Roth IRA.

The thing to keep in mind, though, is that not all IRAs are created equal. You can fill your portfolio with good investments, or you can fill your portfolio with bad investments—just as with any kind of investment scenario. You need to vet all the investments affiliated with any IRA plan you're looking at before you put your money there.

Wherever you put your money, though, pay attention to your rate of return. Look at the numbers at least once a year and make adjustments if necessary.

Self-Directed IRAs

I recommend putting your money into a self-directed IRA, which just means you get to be in charge of all of your investments. Everything else is exactly the same. It can be a self-directed traditional or a self-directed Roth IRA. All the rules and regulations are the same.

You can move your current IRA plan over to a self-directed IRA plan at any time, or you can mix things up and only move some of your current IRA balances over to a self-directed plan. You can have multiple IRAs—you just can't exceed that cumulative contribution limit.

If you do the self-directed option, you will likely also save quite a bit of money on fees. When you put your IRA with, say, a broker who is investing your money for you, he will usually be compensated with a percentage of your growth, which could be upwards of thousands and tens of thousands of dollars per year. If your money is in a self-directed IRA, you're not going to be paying percentages—you'll most likely be looking at flat fees for administration costs, which will be in the hundreds per year.

The big companies like Fidelity and Merrill Lynch all have self-directed options, but you can only self-direct in whatever they sell. If you really want to expand your options, you can find a private third party, such as my friend and colleague Carl Fischer with CamaPlan, who will allow you to fill your investment portfolio with any qualified investment you want.

Buying Real Estate with Your IRA

One of the best things you can do with your IRA investment is to buy houses and have them as part of that portfolio. I will explain why: Let's say you have an IRA with $200,000 in it, and once you hit retirement age, you start withdrawing from that account. On the one hand, let's imagine that money is sitting in a bank account earning 1.5 percent interest because you never read this book, or came to Investor Schooling, and don't know any better. Now let's say you start taking out $6,000 a year, which is an average of $500 a month.

Your account balance is going to go from $200,000 to $194,000, right? Of course, it will. Anything you ever take out is going to be an immediate deduction off the top.

But. Now let's say you've read this book, or you've come to Investor Schooling, and you know a better way to work this. I'm going to teach you that better way right now.

What if you invest that $200,000 into real estate instead? Let's say you buy a building that brings in a minimum of $500 a month in rental income. Assuming that the property value never goes up (which they always do), the value of your IRA is never going to go down. You see, you'll be collecting that $500 a month, which comes to $6,000 a year, and the value of the property—the value of your original investment—is going to stay the same or go up. (It's likely it's going to increase by more than that 1.5 percent you'd be getting from the bank.)

All of that is being held and distributed by your IRA. Once you find the property you want to buy, you call your agent and direct him on the purchase you want made. The agent purchases the property, and now the deed down at the courthouse says "CamaPlan, for the benefit of Jane Smith's IRA." You see, the IRA is a completely separate entity. The IRA owns the property. You are just the beneficiary of the IRA. It's similar to what I've been telling you about LLCs. When I put properties in the name of my LLCs, there's a piece of paper that owns the property. I don't own anything. That's how you need to think of your IRA, too. As the beneficiary, you get the check when you are ready to take the money out. You put money in; you get money out. Everything in between is not in your control . . . sort of. The only control you have is where the money you put in is going to be invested. It's important to understand that.

Either way, though, this is one of the most genius plays you could ever do with an IRA—especially if you are 72 or older and are required to start taking a minimum withdrawal from your account each year. Your tax accountants will tell you the opposite. If you are 72 or older, they will tell you this is not the time to start buying properties. And they are wrong.

If you're still in your working years, you are more likely to be looking at a traditional fix and flip. For instance, say you buy a house for $100,000 and it costs you $35,000 to rehab it. You sell it for $250,000. After you subtract the other $40,000 in miscellaneous costs, you're looking at a profit of around $75,000. (That's a normal real estate deal, by the way. That's what we teach at Investor Schooling all the time.)

You made $75,000 on $135,000. That's a lot of money really fast, and then you take the $210,000 and do another one. There's a guy I know who does a presentation on how much money he's made doing this. He turned his $85,000 Roth IRA into $800,000 in four years, and he is really glad it was a Roth IRA so he doesn't have to pay any taxes on that $715,000 of growth.

The Rules of Investing with a Roth IRA

Now, if you're going to invest with your Roth IRA, there are some important rules you need to follow. Otherwise, you risk disqualifying your entire portfolio and it will revert back to a traditional IRA. Here are the basics:

- You must use a custodial service like CamaPlan. We are good friends with Carl Fischer over there, and I highly recommend him.

- All money and proceeds must flow in and out of your IRA. The check comes from the IRA, the proceeds go back into the IRA. It doesn't go to you and then you write the check to someone else. You cannot do that.
- You cannot benefit financially in any way outside your IRA. This is the one that trips people up because they're thinking they can have a rental property and then decide that they are going to be the manager on the project and then their IRA is going to pay them $10,000 for that. No way. Ain't gonna happen. If you do that, you are going to cause a major problem.
- You should have a property manager for the IRA property, and that manager should be paid out of the IRA. This is another one that's difficult for those who like to keep their own hands on their properties. But if you are managing the property by yourself, there's a chance you are going to become disqualified. You see, the concept of investing inside your IRA is that it is completely hands off. Once it's in your IRA, it no longer belongs to you as an individual. You hand the money to a custodian, the money goes somewhere else, and then that money goes back to the custodian. If you knock on the door and collect the rent, even if you put the check into the IRA, you just touched the money and compromised the integrity of the whole operation. You cannot touch the money. You are not the property manager. You can't be or else you risk disqualifying your entire IRA. And you don't want to do that.
- A disqualified person cannot benefit in any way from your IRA. A disqualified person is typically a relative of yours. In

other words, you can't rent a building inside your IRA to your kid, your mother, your ex-spouse—people such as those. Don't even try it. You will get into trouble. You can't purchase an IRA investment from a disqualified person, either. For example, you can't purchase a house from your mother and put it in your IRA. The seller can't be related to you.

- Any loans used to purchase real estate must be non-recourse loans and cannot be personally guaranteed. At Investor Schooling, we teach you how to do personal guarantees. However, that's just not something you can do with IRAs. If you have an IRA worth $500,000 and you use some to buy a property for $200,000, the seller could still go after the IRA and get his money back for the loan. They can't go after you personally, though. The IRA is its own entity.
- You cannot deduct the mortgage interest or taxes. Duh. You are in a tax-free vehicle. You can't deduct the taxes because you didn't pay any.
- You or your real estate agents cannot live in the property and cannot run a business out of the property. For instance, I couldn't buy a building as part of my IRA portfolio and then rent it to Investor Schooling. It would break the IRA.
- All rents must be deposited into the IRA. This one is the biggest mistake that I see made most often. If you buy a house in your IRA and the rents go into your pocket, you are going to be in trouble.
- You cannot use any personal money to make repairs. This is another one I see people mess up all the time: You put the property in your IRA and then your IRA runs out of money. But you need drywall. So, what do you want to do? You

want to go to Home Depot, take out your card, and buy the drywall. But that is a dangerous thing to do. You are probably going to create a tax problem doing that. Your entire IRA could become disqualified. If repairs need to be made, they must be paid for out of the IRA.

- If you haven't already contributed your $6,000 into your IRA and you are at this point, contribute the $6,000 into your IRA and use that money until it runs out. This is another one people get tripped up on all the time. I don't care if you have to borrow it off a credit card. You can't afford *not* to put that money into an IRA.

I hope by now I have convinced you of the virtues of choosing a self-directed IRA. In this way, you will be able to create wealth many times faster than going the traditional route and guarantee that your best days are yet to come.

How's that for a retirement plan?

CHAPTER 20

Tax Secrets of the Super-Rich

Now that you have a sense of the power of a self-directed IRA, I want to hand you even more resources that you can use in this way. I'm going to share with you some of the top tax secrets of the super-rich. Some of these things you may have heard of—others will completely blow your mind. But even those things you think you know—trust me, you don't know the half of it.

So, let's begin!

First of all, how would you like it if all of your children's toys, clothes, and basic expenses were tax free? Imagine going to your accountant and saying, "Mr. Accountant, I bought my son, Johnny, a PS5. It cost me $600. Can I write that off?" He's going to stare at you for a long time before he starts laughing.

But you can. And I'm going to teach you how. In fact, this strategy is going to allow you to help establish your children's wealth with money that also becomes a tax deduction for you.

But first, I have to talk about what a standard deduction is.

The Standard Deduction

Standard deduction rules were created to simplify tax returns and allow lower-income taxpayers to get some tax relief normally afforded only to the rich who itemize their returns. Average Americans generally couldn't afford—or wouldn't budget—to pay an accountant to itemize their deductions, and the IRS didn't think that was fair. (Imagine the IRS calling something unfair!) So, the IRS came up with the "standard deduction."

For single taxpayers, the standard deduction is currently $12,400; and for married taxpayers filing jointly it is $24,800. That means that you are not taxed on the first $12,400 of your income if you are single, or the first $24,800 of your combined income if you are married.

That's pretty easy to follow, and you have likely been taking this standard deduction for years, if not decades. For instance, if you are married and your combined income is $114,100, the standard deduction is $24,800, which brings your taxable income down to $90,000. And if you make $12,400 or less, then your taxable income is zero dollars and you pay nothing. Simple, right?

Well, now I'm going to teach you how to take advantage of that tax deduction in a brand-new way—a way that you have never heard of before.

Tax-Free Child Rearing

If you have children under the age of 18, how much money per year do you think you're spending on them? Or even your grandkids. I'm talking clothes, toys, video games, bicycles, vacations, and other activities and comforts. Now, what if you could write off $12,400 of those expenses?

You can.

You can pay your children $12,400 a year and let them buy their own stuff. How much in taxes would they have to pay on that $12,400? Zero. If you have a business, how much of that can you deduct from your taxable income? All of it. And you can do this for each of your children—as many as you can afford.

This is real.

And now I'm going to pause here as you let your brain reassemble itself.

Now, you have to understand that you can't just say that your baby granddaughter is an employee and randomly write off that amount. You have to do something to justify your granddaughter as an employee. For instance, you could make a case for her being the new poster child for your business and those are her modeling fees. But it has to be legit.

In order for this to work, however, you also have to have an actual business income you're using to pay your child. But that's easy enough. Let's say you're running a real estate business and you're sending out mailers all the time. You can have your child fold the mailers, put them in envelopes, and put on the stamps. Then you send out those mailers and you get a deal that makes you $15,000. You use that income to pay your kid the $12,400, and then you only have to pay taxes on the remaining $2,600.

Even small children can be real employees. A 7-year-old can do some simple filing for you and shred paper or put stamps on an envelope. And legally, you can pay your employees whatever you want. You just have to be able to show there was a real exchange of services for that payment. So, you pay them $12,400 for the year. It becomes a tax deduction for you, and it is a standard deduction for them.

Since your children are underage, you are the guardian and controller of that money. Yes, little Suzy has $12,400, but you're not giving her the checkbook. Let's say she needs a new wardrobe or even a car for her 16th birthday. You can pay for those things using her own money. It's tax free! Neither of you have to pay taxes on that money. But why stop at toys and other normal purchases? That money can be used for anything, including investing.

If you use this strategy, you don't necessarily have to have your children do a tax return. The laws here are vague. But I would recommend that you do the return just to keep your ducks in a row. It will keep you from getting audited. In fact, if you want to make your paper trail really tight, you can even use a payroll company to pay them.

Coverdell and 529 Savings Accounts

Now, you might have noticed that I didn't include school expenses in the discussion above. That's because there is an entirely different vehicle you will want to use for those. These are education savings accounts, or ESAs. There are two kinds: a Coverdell and a 529. All of the money you put into those accounts is a tax deduction for you and has to be used for education expenses. (Anything spent on non-education expenses will have a 10 percent penalty.)

With a Coverdell, you can put $2,000 per child or per beneficiary per year into that account. Once it's in there, the money can be invested into anything, including the stock market and real estate.

This is cool because you can grow that money pretty quickly with those kinds of investments, and the growth will also be tax-free.

With a 529, you basically put it in a savings account and it is limited to certain conversative investments. However, you can put in up to $15,000 per year. That's really helpful, especially if you have a lot of money and you want to put it away faster for college.

In both of these accounts, the money has to be used by the time the child turns 30. But let's say your child doesn't need that money for college. Maybe your son got scholarships and everything was paid, or maybe your daughter never went to college in the first place. Then what?

Well, you can transfer the beneficiary to another child. If there isn't someone else in the lineup, you can use that money on other things, but there will be a 10 percent penalty on any funds that aren't used for school expenses—either for college or private schooling.

Personally, I think it's awesome that these accounts can be used for private schools because those expenses are not generally tax deductible. But if you put it in an education savings account first, that money automatically becomes tax deductible, and then you just make the tuition payments from that account.

Pay for College with Your IRA

You can also use your standard Roth IRA to pay for college expenses. A lot of people don't know that, but it's true. Withdrawals from IRAs are exempt from withdrawal penalties if the funds are used for qualified educational fees, including tuition fees, books, room, and board. It is no different from the Coverdell or the 529.

In fact, in some ways it's even better. With a Roth, if the kid doesn't go to college, who cares? All that money just becomes a nest egg. It's the beginning of the legacy you are leaving behind. You don't have to play the game of finding another beneficiary or having to pay penalties on non-education expenses. So, you definitely want to use this as a resource for paying for your children's school expenses.

I suggest structuring your ESA investments this way:

First, make the $6,000 maximum contribution to the Roth. If you use the $12,400 you paid to your child, then you're using tax-free money to do that, and you're still the custodian of those funds because your child is under 18.

Second, make the $2,000 maximum contribution to a Coverdell, also using that $12,400. This still leaves an additional $4,400 in your child's "expense account." You can use that to spend on their normal every-day purchases or, if you really want to put money into a 529, you can put that money there.

I recommend maxing out your contributions to your child's Roth IRA and a Coverdell before you go with the 529, though, because of the freedom and the earning potential those accounts give you. Both of them let you invest in anything you want to.

Health Savings Account

You can also use a health savings account—an HSA—to reduce your tax liabilities. This is an account you can put money into that can then be applied to your medical expenses, including dental and vision.

How is this different than a normal savings account? Let me explain.

I have high-deductible insurance. Before my insurance will pay a single dollar toward my medical expenses, I have to pay $7,000 out of pocket. Now, you might be thinking, *Well, at least it's going to count as a tax deduction.*

Wrong. It isn't. Remember that Standard Deduction we were talking about? Well, let's say you go to the doctor and have an MRI that costs $3,000. That's going to be entirely swallowed up in that standard deduction. Unless . . .

This is where the HSA comes in handy. So, now I'm going to explain how it works, why it works, and why you should have one.

The maximum contribution for an HSA is $3,550 if you are an individual, and it is $7,100 for a family. However, in order to qualify for this account, you have to have a high-deductible insurance plan. A high deductible here is defined as being $1,400 or higher. So, if you have a deductible that is any less than that, I suggest you talk to your broker and ask for a higher deductible immediately so that you can reap the benefits of using this vehicle. You see, all of your contributions to the HSA are tax deductible—*beyond* your standard deductions.

If you put $7,100 in there, every penny of that can be deducted from your taxable income. Any of the money used from that account for a medical expense is tax free. So, going back to that $3,000 MRI, even though you can't itemize it on your tax return and write it off, you already wrote off the $7,100 that you used to pay for the MRI. In addition, your contributions are carried over from year to year. If you put $7,100 in this year and have $0 in medical expenses, next year you could put in another $7,100 and have a total of $14,200 in your HSA. The money grows tax free, and there is no penalty for non-qualified withdrawals after age 65.

Hmmm . . . What does this sound like? An IRA!

Yes, this is essentially another IRA. And listen to this: You can use your HSA to invest in anything you want, just as if it were a self-directed IRA. You can invest in stocks, real estate, gold, silver—

almost anything you can imagine. The rules are the same as the IRA, and the same restrictions apply.

Live Rich, Be Rich

And there you have it—some of the tax secrets of the super-rich. As you implement these strategies, you won't just be mirroring their strategies; you will be carving your own path to massive wealth and leaving a legacy for your children as you go.

CHAPTER 21

Understanding College Loans

Speaking of education expenses, remember in 2006 and 2007 when everyone called the banks predatory lenders because they were inflating the prices of houses and giving out loans at 125 percent of what the homes were actually worth? Those were not predatory loans. As an adult, you at least have some financial knowledge. You can understand, at some level, the agreement you're entering into with your bank and whether or not it's a good contract. If you still choose to sign your name on that line, then part of that responsibility and blame falls to you.

Now imagine 17- or 18-year-old kids coming to that same table. These are kids who have likely either never worked a day in their lives, or the best job they've ever had was flipping burgers at a fast-food joint. They've likely never paid a bill, and they've certainly never had to figure out how to keep the lights on and food on the table. These are kids!

They know nothing about money.

They know nothing about interest.

These kids come to the same lenders' tables, only they're not trying to buy a house. They're trying to get money so that they can go to college. They're doing exactly what they've been told their entire lives to do by parents, teachers, and society. They're barely making a choice at all. Then, they have these papers put in front of them and they're asked to sign. The only thing standing between them and their future is putting their name on that line.

So, they sign.

Because they believe the lie.

One of the biggest lies we are being told in this country is that we need to go to college in order to get a good job and that we need to take out student loans in order to make all that happen.

Let's talk about that.

As of March 31, 2021, there was $1.7 trillion in total US student loan debt across 42.9 million Americans holding that debt.[6] When you do the math, that averages out to be almost $40,000 per person. The average student loan payment on these loans is $393.[7]

These are all averages. This means there are those with substantially more debt—and higher payments—than this. There are kids who went to college for less than a year who are still paying off a few thousand dollars in loans, and there are doctors and lawyers who still owe upwards of $150,000 on their student loans. In March 2019 (before COVID), the Department of Education reports that only 56 percent of all student loan debts are actively being repaid, while the other 44 percent are either on hold or in default.[8] Robert Kiyosaki, the author of *Rich Dad Poor Dad*, said, "In my opinion, the United States and many western countries have a financial disaster coming, caused by our educational system's failure to adequately provide a realistic financial education for their students."

This crisis in only going to get worse. Tuition prices are steadily going up, year after year. The U.S. Bureau of Labor and Statistics reported that the Consumer Price Index (CPI) of basic needs, such as housing and food, went up 22.8 and 31 percent, respectively, between 2003 and 2014. Compare that to the CPI of college tuition, which went up 79.5 percent in that same period of time.

College is Not the Problem

Going to college in and of itself is not the problem. It may or may not be a good path for your children, depending on what they want to do. But the loans are a huge problem.

I'm here to tell you that student loans are the most predatory loans you can possibly get. They are predatory in every way. They aren't just targeting the youth with little experience. They target you—the parents—too.

When my son went to college, his mother and stepfather signed the papers for what they thought was a college grant—free money for my son's college expenses. They signed all the paperwork and sent him on his way to school. Then, a few weeks after classes started, my son got a bill for $12,000. They all looked at each other and said, "What is this?! This was supposed to be a grant!" It was a loan after all. I'm telling you, that was no accident. Three intelligent people—my son, his mother, and his step-father—all looked over that paperwork before they signed. It was a cleverly disguised contract.

That's how predatory this institution is.

Student Loan Forgiveness

That's not the only clever disguise out there. Have you heard of college loan forgiveness? This is what you're told:

If you become a public-school teacher in a low-income area, there is college loan forgiveness.

If you join the military, there is forgiveness.

If you apply for the income-based repayment plan, there is forgiveness.

If you get a public service, government, or non-profit job, there is forgiveness.

You've likely heard some of these rumors. Now, let me tell you the truth about them:

If you become a public-school teacher in a low-income area, you may qualify for up to $17,500 of your loans to be forgiven, and only after you have worked (and presumably been paying on those loans) for at least five years. On the surface, it sounds as if all of the loans—whether they come to $10,000 or $100,000—will be forgiven. Nope. *Up to* $17,500 means that it could be even less than that. I certainly hope no one is making career choices based on those promises, considering that the average cost of just one year of school as an in-state student at a public college is over $25,000[3] and teachers are known for being underpaid.

If you join the military, the amount of loan forgiveness is dependent on your level of rank. Now, I'm not sure which rank offers the greatest amount of forgiveness, but I'm sure it's not Private.

If you apply for the income-based repayment plan, there is not forgiveness—there is refinancing. That's not the same thing. Not by a long shot. The idea is that you only have to pay 15 percent of your discretionary income toward your loan. I don't know about you, but most people in the world don't have any discretionary income. They barely have enough to pay their bills each week, and now they're told they're going to have to come up with a certain number of dollars that are supposedly "extra" in order to make their loan payment. The actual number is based on a generic, universal formula—it's not determined by the unique and personal details of each person's financial situation.

Finally, if you get a public service, government, or non-profit job, you will receive forgiveness on the remaining balance of your Direct Loans (and Direct Loans only) after you've made 120 qualifying monthly payments on them while working full-time. That's ten years of payments. In most instances, you're likely to have paid off your loans by that time anyway.[9]

Do you want to know the only real student loan forgiveness program?

Death.

That's the only one.

You can't even claim bankruptcy to get out of repaying your student loans. Imagine being in a financial situation in your life that is so dire that you're willing to file Chapter 11. I personally know what that means. I can't imagine going through that personal h*** to wipe your slate clean—only to have it still not be clean.

Student loans are the absolute worst thing we can do for our children's financial futures—and we're doing it to them at the very beginning of their adult lives. If you haven't made this mistake already, please never, ever allow your child to sign their name on a student loan application.

If You Have to Do it Anyway

Now, I know it's not enough for me to beg you never to allow this to happen to your children. You won't be so easily persuaded. The reality is that you're still going to send your child to college and you may not have any other choice than to use student loans to make that happen.

Okay, fine.

Then I will at least give you the knowledge you need so that you know how to structure those loans so that they don't end up destroying lives.

I have to note here, however, that this assumes you're going to use the guaranteed student loan programs, which are Federal- or state-funded loans backed by government funds. I highly recommend that you don't use this program and use some other source of loan if possible, such as a personal loan, equity in your home, a credit card—anything else. But assuming that you decide you have no other choice than to go down the route of getting a government guaranteed loan, I'm going to tell you the absolute best way for you to structure that loan.

The Problem with Student Loans

The biggest problem with student loans is something called "deferred interest." This means that you don't have to pay anything for a period of time, but the interest never stops building. PayPal has this setup with their six-months deferred interest program. So, if you borrow $1,000 from your PayPal Credit account and you pay it back within that six-month period, you owe them zero dollars in interest. You just pay $1,000 back. If you pay back only $999 in that six-month period, however, and that remaining $1 rolls over into six months and one day, you now owe the entire amount of interest that accrued on that $1,000 over the six-month period.

It's not quite the same with your student loans, but it's similar.

Your children are told they can borrow $50,000 at a differed interest rate of 6 percent and they don't have to make a single payment while they're in college. That sounds like a dream come true, right?

Not so much.

By the time you've read this far in this book, I hope you understand how compound interest can be a powerful tool for building large amounts of wealth over time. But the opposite is also true. When it comes to your debts—student loans, especially—compound interest can work against you. For most student loans with differed interest, all of the interest just piles up for four years—or however long it takes to graduate—and is capitalized at the end of the grace period, which means it's added to the principal balance of the loan. So, if your daughter gets a $50,000 loan today and then defers all the payments on that loan for four years, it will accumulate $12,000 in interest, which will then be added to the principal balance when she graduates.

That's how a $50,000 loan becomes a $62,000 loan.

That's a 24 percent increase! Your child hasn't even done anything yet. She's just been sitting in a desk, learning outdated information and being indoctrinated for four years, and now she owes $12,000 more than what he borrowed. She'll be paying interest on interest for the lifetime of her loan payments.

Oh, but let's not forget about the grace period. Your child graduates college in June and the lender is so gracious to give her until September to make her first payment. It's so kind of them to let our children enjoy the last summer of their freedom before they enter into decades of financial servitude on their student loans.

If they pay the loan back in ten years instead of the normal twenty, the monthly payment is going to be $688.33 a month. By the time the debt is paid, the total amount of interest paid will be $32,599—bringing the total amount paid on the $50,000 loan to be $82,599. That's 65 percent more than the original loan.

The numbers are mind blowing. You probably suspected they would be bad, but did you realize they would be this bad? Do you think they explain the numbers this way to your children when they're handing them the pen so they can sign? Absolutely not. If that doesn't make you angry, I don't know what does. I wish this chapter could be mandatory reading for every child going to college.

So, your kids are borrowing $50,000 to go to college so they can get a good job, and then they graduate and get a job serving tables because they can't get a job in their field, but they're still on the hook to pay the full $82,599.

It doesn't have to look like that. I'm going to tell you what to do instead.

The Best Way to Structure a Student Loan

First, I'm going to ask you a question, and I need you to answer honestly: If your child graduated college and then couldn't get a job, would you make that loan payment? Knowing what you know about student loans and how the interest is always accruing, even while in deferment, and how devastating it is to one's personal credit to leave those loans unpaid, are you going to make those payments on behalf of your kid? Probably so.

Now, I understand not everyone will, and not everyone can afford to. If you know you would, though, my advice is to do it immediately, as soon as that loan is taken out. You will lower your total loan cost by thousands and thousands of dollars if you pay the interest before the interest capitalizes after graduation.

If you start making payments immediately, your payment will only be $555.10 a month for the lifetime of the loan. So, as soon your child gets the loan, *you* make the loan payment of $555.10 the very next month. Then you're making payments on a $50,000 loan instead of a $62,000 loan. The odds are very high that you're going to be the one paying the loans anyway. If your child graduates and gets a job, great! But it happens far too often that graduates end up working at a restaurant or a gas station, and then they can't make these payments. Even if they defer the loan or if they do an income-based repayment plan that allows them to make a smaller payment or pay the loan back over more time, the interest is still growing! The longer it takes to repay that loan, the more that is going to be paid in interest. The financial weight that is crouching over your child's future just continues to get heavier and heavier and heavier.

Listen, I'm not trying to degrade your children or discourage them at all. I'm just suggesting that, statistically, this is a possible reality for them. Therefore, I'm trying to give you a game plan that will help them tremendously.

So, if you start making that $555.10 payment immediately and keep paying on it while your children are in school, the total interest would only be $16,612 over ten years—$15,987 less than if you waited to start making payments until after graduation. That's about half the interest. The total payments would come to $66,612 over ten years instead of $82,599. Compare that to the $62,000 they would owe when they graduated before they even started making any payments. That puts you so far ahead!

Hopefully, you won't be the one making those payments all of that time. Ideally, your children will graduate and get jobs and be able take over the payments as soon as they graduate. Imagine handing over a $555.10 payment to them instead of a $688.33 payment. That's a difference of over $130 a month. That's a huge difference—especially to a 22-year-old kid.

If there's a chance you're going to be paying those loans anyway, even if it's just for a time, why not do it like this? Not only will it save you money and them money, but it's going to give your children a better chance in life. This is my strongest suggestion to anyone. In fact, if you can get a loan at 6 percent and you have $50,000 in the bank, why not keep the $50,000 in the bank that you were going to use to pay for college and take out the loan instead? Pay it back the way I've outlined here, and then use that $50,000 cash to invest in something else that's going to give you 10 to 15 percent back on your money and make that college loan payment for you. You'll come out far ahead of that $66,612 over the next ten years.

I know you're probably thinking, *Larry, you just told me you hate college loans, and now you're telling me to use them for the benefit of me and my children!*

I promise, I'm not talking out of both sides of my mouth here. The key is to manage the loan exactly as I've outlined in this chapter. Also, I did mention—and still stand behind—the fact that this should still be your last option when it comes to loans. If you can get a mortgage or a personal loan for the $50,000 at a 6 percent or lower interest rate, then do it that way instead.

I'm telling you, I've been on this planet for about six decades, and I've learned a lot of things along the way. Some of these are complicated concepts that took me years to learn. Some of them are simple concepts that took me seconds to comprehend. So often, those simple concepts are those revolving around money, and it blows my mind that there are so many people out there who don't know them. It's not that they don't understand them—they simply do not know them because they've never had the privilege of coming across this information. These are simple concepts that a child could grasp—if only that child had the opportunity to hold them.

Please, please, please—give your child that opportunity. It won't just change the amount they owe on student loans each month. I guarantee it will change their entire lives.

CHAPTER 22

How to Thrive in a Bad Economy

When COVID hit in the spring of 2020, it was a pretty somber moment at my school (InvestorSchooling.com). Usually, I go to class and get up in front of the room and start by getting everyone laughing. But that night, I went in and everything was quiet. It was as if I was at a funeral. There were some people there who had already lost a lot of money—including myself.

The COVID crisis caused the third-largest loss in the history of the stock market, and no one could have predicted or prepared for that. When you wake up and you see the reports and you tally up the losses—it's a very sobering moment. It is what it is, and you can't do anything about it. The two most defining moments are what you decide that you're going to do next—and what you decided to do before it ever happened in the first place.

I don't know what you were doing in 2008, but I was holding millions of dollars in real estate investments. I was living on borrowed luck, and it ran out fast. I lost everything, practically overnight. I filed bankruptcy and had to start completely over. But that wasn't the end of everything. It was the beginning of something else.

Since then, I have had my credit score as high as 805 (the last time I checked, it was a 725). My available credit on credit cards is now over $660,000. I have accumulated many assets, and I am worth well over a million dollars again. Things have completely turned around for me.

But I'm not stupid—not like I was before 2008. I didn't rebuild *again*—I rebuilt *differently*. After having lived through a market crash a couple times, I now understand it's not a matter of if but a matter of when it will happen again. So, I have simultaneously been building and preparing at the same time. I'm in this for the long game.

Here, I'm going to teach you the strategies you need in order to survive, if necessary, for the two-to five years it takes for things to bounce back after the market crashes—or even allow you to make money when the rest of the world is standing in a breadline. There's a reason I made more money over the course of COVID in 2020 than in any year of my entire life.

Leverage Your Credit

First of all, when things start to go south, you need to either have cash or quick access to cash.

If you don't already have money stowed away somewhere, one of the best ways to protect yourself in a downturn is to make sure you have some available credit. It is going to be powerful. You can use that credit to purchase assets that will make you money. I'm talking about houses and other investments—not furniture or cars or other kinds of depreciating assets. Even if I had to pay 25 percent interest (which I'm not—I'm just using this as an example), as long as I'm purchasing an asset that is going to make me more than that interest, who cares? If I'm buying a house, then either my tenants are going to be paying that interest or I am getting that money back when I sell the property.

One of my students bought a property with credit cards (see *Chapter 11: How to Buy a House with Credit Cards*). He flipped that house and made a $27,000 profit after the credit cards had been paid off. The entire transaction happened in two months. Sixty days, $27,000 in profit. Not bad! That property cost him nothing out of his own pocket because he borrowed all the money from his credit cards. And once the house was sold and his credit card was paid off, he could just rinse and repeat the entire process. So, what was his true return? It's infinite.

If you play the game right, you can do this, too—even in a bad economy.

The Credit Dilemma in a Bad Economy

But wait a minute—isn't it going to be harder to get credit cards in a bad economy? You bet it is. That's why you need to get them when you can—and why you need to be smart about the lines of credit you're getting.

In 2008 and 2009, banks started calling loans even though people were paying on time. There was no problem, no issue—banks just called the loans because they were getting worried about their entire books of business. A manager would hand somebody a stack of papers and say, "Call these people, and tell them we are calling their loans; send them letters." The bank didn't even look at the loans. They didn't care. They just took a block of loans and canceled them, trying to save their own skins. And it was perfectly legal. They can do that whenever they want to.

Your creditors are always assessing you—to see if you have any late payments, if you are doing anything that's weird, or if you're borrowing too much money. In good times, lenders give you a lot of slack. For example, there's something called "credit card skating," which is when you take, say, a 1 percent line of credit and use it to pay off another line of credit that is charging you 10 percent interest; and then, when that 1 percent card runs out, you use another 1 percent line of credit to pay that off. If creditors see that behavior during good times, they might just look the other way. But if they're starting to sweat over what's going to happen with the economy, they might call you up and say, "Listen, we see what you're doing, and you're high risk. Your credit limit was $20,000, but now it is $5,000."

All of a sudden, they are looking for reasons to make your line of credit as small as possible.

When this happens, it can hurt. Not only will you have less credit available to you, but the credit that you've used is going to have a greater impact on your credit score. Let me explain. Let's say you owe $5,000 on a $20,000 limit. You've used 25 percent of the credit available to you. That's not too bad. But if they suddenly change your limit to $5,000, now you've used 100 percent of the credit available to you (to better understand how this affects your credit score, see *Chapter 7: The Truth About Credit Scores*). To make matters worse, let's say you pay $1,000 on your account to lessen the damage. All of a sudden, the creditor is probably going to lower your limit down to $4,000. The problem doesn't go away, and now you have an even smaller line of credit.

Now, it's highly unlikely that your home mortgage or a HELOC (Home Equity Line of Credit) will be called. That's probably not going to happen. But a standard line of credit? Yeah, they might call that. They're not going to do that just at any time, but when the economy looks like it's heading for a brick wall at high speed, it's likely going to happen.

So, you want to be careful about where you have your money.

Economy-Proof Credit

In fact, I am going to recommend you get a HELOC right now—regardless of whether or not you're in a downturn. Any day, any time—if you have any equity in your house whatsoever, get a HELOC. When you have that in place, you can write a check and give yourself a loan when you need it. And if you never write the check, you're not paying anything on the interest on the HELOC. It just sits there as a line of credit, available to you whenever you need it. It may cost you five hundred bucks to open the account, but after that, it won't cost you anything—and having that security in place is worth the nominal fees to get it.

I love this strategy. It lets you have access to money when a good investment deal comes along—and frankly, not only when a good deal comes along. If you happen to be out of work or the economy is struggling and you need to write yourself a check, you could survive on that HELOC a couple months or years, depending on how much home equity you have.

If you see the economy heading for a turn, time is of the essence! Even if you plan on staying in your house long-term and aren't worried about the short-term value of your home over the next few years, the potential value of your HELOC will go down during that time, and that will be a lost opportunity.

Years ago, I worked for Crazy Eddie, the flamboyant electronics retailer who made a name for himself in the 80s. (The guy was crazier than I am.) I was one of his store managers, and one day, there was a big article in the paper about how he was looking for credit. He called all of us managers into a meeting because he was afraid that the article may have made him look bad. He said, "You guys may have read somewhere that we're looking for credit. Well, I want you to understand that we're always looking for credit. Because when you need credit, you can't get it. When you don't need it, you can."

That really stayed with me, and it's completely true. I agree with Eddie—get it while you can! It's a rule I live by, and you should, too. If your credit score is all the way up to 850, use it and make it 720. It will be the best 130 points you ever "spent," because then you're going to have more available credit and be able to make investments you otherwise wouldn't have been able to.

For example, when COVID hit, my house was worth about $440,000 and I owed $280,000. I immediately secured a HELOC for the entire value of my equity because I knew the value of the property might go down in the short-term. And as soon as I grabbed that HELOC, I had it. It wasn't going to be called or cancelled, the line of credit wasn't going to be lowered. It was just sitting there, ready for me to use it if I needed it. Even if the value of my home went down to, let's say, $380,000 and I still owed $280,000—I would still have the entire value of my previous equity available to me.

You may not care about the HELOC if you've been considering moving in the next few years. But if you can see a crash coming, don't wait "the next few years." Now is the time to move. When 2008 happened, it really didn't get bad until a few years later. The worst year of that crisis was 2011. So, even if everything hit the fan today, it's going to be a minute before things really hit rock bottom. When things start to go south, that is the best time to move or sell your house if you've been thinking about it. Do it—not because you are panicking, but because you want to get the most money for your house while you can.

Remember: The view from your current position is the best it's going to be for a while if things are on their way down.

Stash Your Cash

Again, it's vital that you either have cash or access to cash through credit.

When COVID hit, one of the first things I did was write checks against my 0 percent and 1 percent lines of credit and stash that cash. I had to pay interest on that cash, but it kept the creditor from lowering my credit limit, and I had cash to lean on, just in case.

Is maxing out my credit limit going to affect my credit score? Yes. But what do I need my credit score for? If the economy starts going south, what does it matter? I am not going to be buying another car. My primary residence already has a mortgage and a HELOC. Any loans I have on investment properties are held by private lenders—and all of those properties have renters in them paying the mortgages and then some.

Don't worry about your credit score unless you need to get a mortgage for your primary residence or buy a car. If I have a 550 credit score and I am not going to get a mortgage or a car, do I look any different? Is anything different in my life because my credit score is 550? No. Be prepared for what's best *for* you, not what's best for the *perception* of you.

The worst thing that could happen is that you may have to lower your tenants' rents to the point where you're just breaking even and making sure all your private lenders are still getting paid. But you definitely don't have to worry about those loans getting called.

By the way, that's another great reason to use private lenders—the loans will never be called. The properties have equity in them, and the renters are paying my mortgage, so I am not worried about them. And the lenders aren't worried about them because even if I default, they just get a great deal on an investment property. It's all good, even if I just have to survive through the two to five years it might take for the economy to bounce back again.

Safety in Silver

One of the smartest things you can do is start buying silver. I am not talking about a silver fund. I am talking about actual silver. I probably have close to $60,000 worth of silver in a private safe, according to today's prices. I didn't buy it all at once. I bought it a little bit at a time, and I'm still buying it. Usually, I buy one 10-ounce bar a month, which costs me about $250, depending on the price per ounce. But I buy a lot more than that any time silver is below $20 per ounce.

I want you to start doing the same thing. Buy one bar a month, and then just put it away. This is for your protection. If you have the physical metal, it gives you a guaranteed safety net.

Let's say, for example, that the whole world goes bad and, all of a sudden, your credit cards get cut and you don't have any other lines of credit because you didn't take my advice. Then you lose your job, if you had one. You can't buy anything, and now you have to make decisions *right now*. You have to decide whether or not to keep your house or your car, or to file for bankruptcy and completely trash your credit. Those are the types of decisions that may come up in a scenario like this.

Then you remember that you did take *some* of my advice and you have a bunch of silver stashed away! You decide now is the time to dip into that reserve. But how do you sell it? How do you liquidate it into cash? Now, let's say it's worth $35 an ounce on the open market. That sounds nice, but you're not going to get $35 an ounce for it. Your best bet is to go into a jewelry store or a gold-buying place. If you go to a reputable jewelry store, you can get up to 80 or 90 percent of spot.

You need to be savvy, though. Some places will try to give you half spot, and you want to avoid them. You do not want to sell to those places. So first, you need to know what your silver is worth and be ready to walk if the deal isn't worth it.

I had a bunch of silver in 2008 and 2009 that I had paid $7 an ounce for. When silver hit $50, I decided to sell my stash. I went to a jewelry store, and the guy there gave me $43 an ounce for it. That was an acceptable difference. We shook hands, and I made a ton of money. That wasn't a bad deal.

I hope you're starting to see how silver can be your safety net. If nothing else, it's a good place to start making sure that you have something in case you need it.

Another benefit of the silver is that if anything ever happens to me, my children know where to find it. They can go and get it right out of my safe deposit box, and it immediately passes on from me to them—totally tax free. This is stuff you are hiding. No one knows about it. It doesn't show up on any of your asset sheets. It never has to go through probate or anything.

All of this is also true for gold, by the way. I mean, it doesn't really matter what you invest in. Personally, I like silver because I can buy a bunch of bars of silver for the price of one bar of gold, and I like having it because it looks cool. I open up my safe and just seeing it gives me a little thrill. That's all. I also believe that silver doubles in value faster than gold, but that's not necessarily true. It just seems that way to me. So, it really doesn't matter what you buy—as long as you're buying something. Whatever it is you're going to buy, buy it! Then put it away and hold onto it. It will feel so good just knowing it's there—exactly where you need it when you need it.

No Cash, No Credit—Now What?

Now, let's say you decided not to take any of my advice here. The market starts to crash, and you're short on cash, and you start losing all of your normal avenues of credit. Now what? Well, all is not lost. There are still a few tricks you can pull out of your sleeve.

First of all, I have given you many, many strategies in this book on how to invest with other people's money. Granted, it's probably going to be a little tougher to find investors during hard times. But as long as you can bring something to the table, you will always have the option of using a hard-money lender. The good ones aren't going to go anywhere, even in a down economy.

Second of all, there are unique instances in which you can get in on an asset with zero money down, period.

For example, have you ever heard of buying properties "subject to"? I'm not going to go into it super deep here (you can learn about it at InvestorSchooling.com), but basically, this is when you take over someone else's mortgage payments on a property. When the economy starts to tank, there will be a lot of people who get stuck in their house payments and just want a way out.

There may be people who can't pay their mortgages anymore, and there may be people who can't sell their houses—and these are exactly the people you're looking for if you're interested in a "subject to" property. Those properties may be something that, last week, were worth $120,000 and today they are worth $100,000 and the owner still owes $100,000. They just want out, and they need to move. There's an opportunity there for you to take over the mortgage payment and basically take the property for free.

I did a number of these in the years following 2008—I have done these every year since. After a crash, you'll see these kinds of deals popping up all over the place. But they're hard to find when the economy is doing well.

So, how do you find these deals? It's easier than you think. You will be in casual conversation with someone, and that person might mention how he can't afford his mortgage payment anymore because he lost his job or because he's getting a divorce and he can't sell his home because it's worth more than his mortgage. That's when it's time to start talking about "subject to" properties. It will be a win-win. Once you sign the deal, you can immediately put someone else in there (a tenant) to pay the mortgage for you, and you will even be making a monthly profit on the rent. It becomes a stable income for you, even in the middle of a market crash.

Plant in Many Soils

That last strategy I want to talk about is to have money in different places. Don't put all your eggs in one basket, so to speak. Remember that whole chapter on why it's important to have LLCs (see *Chapter 9: LLCs—The Credit Multiplier*)? This can make a big difference for you when you're looking at large-scale financial unpredictability. I, Larry Steinhouse, don't own any of my assets. How many cars do I own? Zero. How many houses do I own? Zero. How many houses do my LLCs own? Zero.

That last one probably surprised you. But every one of my houses is its own entity called a trust. If anything happens to any of my properties, they are isolated from each other. The nice thing about them being isolated is that when there is an economic nightmare, I can then decide what to do with those properties, one by one. I can work each one separately from every other property. No one can sue me or call in my debts and grab up all my properties at once because they don't exist together.

It's the same for all my assets. I have three LLCs and three separate businesses. Each one of those businesses is its own entity and has its own credit score. This is important in an economic downturn. If worst comes to worst and I need to cut some losses, each of my assets is protected individually. If one becomes a mess, I still have two. If two become a mess, I still have one. And my properties are protected from messes altogether.

Where I live, there is a popular restaurant in a neighboring small town. The owner is losing his gigantic $3 million house at the Jersey Shore. We were talking, and he told me he just can't afford to pay his mortgage anymore—business isn't as good as it used to be. I said, "Aren't you worried you are going to lose your restaurant?" He looked at me like I was crazy. He said, "Why? That's a separate entity."

I just smiled. I knew the answer before he even said it. I knew he was a smart guy. I laughed and said, "I know what you did."

So, this guy is losing his house *while* he is running one restaurant—which is its own separate entity—and opening up another restaurant as another entity across town. His business is completely safe. Do you know why? Each entity is completely separate, with its own credit score and own books.

These are the kinds of things you need to do and learn in order to prepare for what's coming.

Joy Cometh in the Morning

The good news is that when these catastrophes come, you can be confident that they will be temporary problems. There is no doubt in my mind that is true. I've seen the stock market and the economy bounce too many times to believe otherwise. But the problem is that no one knows exactly how temporary they will be. We can't predict how long they will last.

If it lasts a month, it might just be a blip. If it last two months, it is going to be a speed bump. If it goes any further than that, there are going to be some major repercussions. The best thing you can do is prepare yourself for every possibility.

And here it is, the bottom line: In the worst-case scenario, all you need is a few great strategies to keep yourself afloat for the two to five years it will take for the economy to bounce back. Are you going to have pain when it happens? Heck yeah. I had some pain when the COVID crisis first hit the market, for sure—and 2008 was not kind to me.

But even though you have that pain, if you have been smart enough to prepare ahead of time, then once you come out on the other side—oh man, what a position you'll be in.

Conclusion

Be a Legend

Okay, this is the last chapter. The book is done. What's next? Now is the time to decide how you are going to live your life. Are you going to be that mouse in the maze, or are you going to be the one who places the cheese at the end? Are your dreams going to be fulfilled, or are you going to make someone else's dreams come true? Are you going to be the one who makes the stockholders rich, or are you going to be the stockholder collecting profits at the top?

If you're feeling a fire from the things I've given you in this book, don't just close these pages and tuck them away. It was never my intention just to give you the warm fuzzies. Don't make the mistake of thinking that this information is just a blank check you can cash any time you want to. It's not. Not because someone is going to take it away—but because you will forget how important it is. Right now, you feel a passion. Tomorrow, it will time to do laundry and live your normal life again. It will be so easy to do nothing. As easy as breathing.

Don't leave this conversation without taking action.

Call me.

Message me.

Go to InvestorSchooling.com and become a student.

Get a mentor.

Make an investment.

Do *something*.

I have had people pay me thousands of dollars for my program and then never show up. Don't get me wrong, thanks for the money. I love money! But that is only a small part of my dream—a small part of my why. I want to help people. I want to help you.

I've vowed never to accept people's money unless I'm honestly helping them. I live by that.

In fact, my friend Mike came to me a while back and said he wanted to get into real estate to make some extra money. We sat down for some one-on-one coaching, and I began by trying to get to the core of his *why*—the thing that would drive him to his success. I asked him, "Why do you want to make money?"

"I want to record my songs," he said.

"Tell me more about that," I said.

His posture immediately changed. His eyes lit up and his hands became animated as he told me about his love for making music and how he couldn't wait to get the recording equipment he needed to be able to record his art.

I appreciated his passion, but I was still a little confused. "Mike, what does making music have to do with buying real estate?" I asked.

"Because I need to come up with the money to buy the recording equipment."

I blinked. "Mike, why don't you just save yourself some time and skip the real estate and go right to buying the recording equipment?" I asked.

The purpose of our coaching session immediately changed. By the end of the hour, he had a pretty good blueprint on how to make his dream come true *years* faster than he thought was ever possible. Soon thereafter, he had that equipment, and he's now in the process of recording his music. I can't wait to listen to his recordings!

To me, Mike is one of my most successful students—even though I never took a dime from him and he hasn't made a dime from real estate or stock options. That's because it's not about the money—it's about the *why*. It's about living! Mike, my friends, understands what it means to live. He isn't putting his life on the back burner until he "figures it out." He's out there doing it. He's making himself into a legend as I write this. I commend him for that.

Now let me tell you about Todd.

Todd heard about Investor Schooling, and he came to me asking to come on as one of my students. He started telling me how he's always wanted to be in real estate, and he asked to sign up for my course. The words he was saying should have been music to my ears. But they weren't. They were all wrong. It wasn't what he said, but how he said it. There was nothing in his demeanor that seemed to agree with what he was saying. He spoke softly and looked bored. There was zero energy coming from him.

I shook my head, looked him the eyes, and said, "I don't think you'll be a good student."

He said, "You don't understand. I can afford you. I will pay you full price!"

I said, "Yeah, I know, but you should keep your money, Todd. I'm telling you—you're not going to be a good student."

See, my first goal was to help him. And I didn't think I could. I just didn't believe he had that x-factor that would allow him to succeed in my course.

Well, he didn't agree, and he refused to give up. He persevered and he pushed until I saw enough fire in him to agree to take him on. It was not without hesitation, though, and I still had my doubts about this guy. I went home to my wife and threw up my hands and said, "I just took this guy's money, and I just hope it works out."

Let me tell you—I've never seen anyone move as fast as Todd moved. During our first coaching session, he told me about a book he started writing two years ago. I said, "Two years ago? Then where is it?"

He hemmed and hawed about "Maybe it's not good enough," and "It's all been said before."

I cut him off and said, "Todd, finish the book. Publish it. Someone is waiting for it." That was the end of his stalling. He hit the ground running after that and knocked it out as fast as he could. As of this writing, the book has been finished, and he honored me with the privilege of writing the foreword. (It's also funny to note that the first chapter is on perseverance—which he definitely put into action when he persevered to become my student!)

Todd's book is a permanent stamp in the universe. That makes him a legend. I wrote the foreword to that book, so if I die tomorrow, I die as a legend, too.

It's those kinds of experiences that really get me going. When my life crosses paths with someone else's and I can make a difference for good—that's what I call living. Those ripple effects go on and on, one life after the other. Who knows who will read Todd's book and go on to make a difference in someone else's life, and on and on from there. It's amazing to think about. That's how it is when you're truly living, though. Life breeds life.

I want you to remember that as you're applying the principles and strategies I've given you. It's about the money, and it's not about the money. Because the money is just a means to an end.

But it's not really an end at all, is it?

No.

It is just the beginning.

About the Author

Larry Steinhouse is a Philadelphia native who has been buying and selling houses since he was 18 years old. He has a passion for investing in profitable properties, lucrative stock options, and teaching others how to do it.

After losing all his wealth—including over $3 million in properties—in the 2008 crash, Larry was determined not to just rebuild his financial security, but to build it differently. He has tirelessly researched the best investment strategies for both current and future financial wealth and how to keep it economy-proof. He is known for his unique money hacks that, on the surface, seem to be the complete opposite of the popular financial counsel of his day. However, these strategies have proven to be the best-kept secrets of the super-rich that have made many people wealthy and are still making people rich today.

In 2014, Larry co-founded Investor Schooling with his business partner, Phil Falcone. The school is a brick-and-mortar real estate and stock options investment school located in Newtown, PA, just outside of Philadelphia. The school welcomes investors (both novice and intermediate level investors) to come learn the tricks of the trade.

In his free time, Larry enjoys shopping for distinctive blazers that mirror his personality, driving one of his sports cars, and continuing to woo his lovely bride, Linda Steinhouse.

Endnotes

1 Wikipedia. "William Post." Last modified October 31, 2020. https://en.wikipedia.org/wiki/William_Post, accessed August 5, 2021.

2 Phillip, Jack. "The Tragic Story of a Kentucky Man Who Won the Lottery." The Epoch Times. https://www.theepochtimes.com/the-tragic-story-of-a-kentucky-man-who-won-the-lottery_2857069.html. March 28, 2019.

3 Engel, Pamela. "21 Lottery Winners Who Blew it All." Insider. https://www.businessinsider.com/lottery-winners-powerball-jackpot-how-much-2016-7. July 8, 2016.

4 https://en.wikipedia.org/wiki/Evelyn_Adams_(lottery_winner)

5 Delaney, Ely. 2020. "'Money Can't Buy Happiness' . . . is a lie." Facebook, November 18, 2020. https://www.facebook.com/elydelaney/posts/10218526908106414.

6 Helhoski, Anna, and Ryan Lane. "Student Loan Debt Statistics: 2021." NerdWallet. https://www.nerdwallet.com/article/loans/student-loans/student-loan-debt. June 15, 2021

7 Farrington, Robert. "What is the Average Student Loan Monthly Payment for US Borrowers?" The College Investor. https://thecollegeinvestor.com/33643/average-student-loan-monthly-payment/. Updated June 27, 2021.

8 Stolba, Stefan Lembo. "Only Half Of All Student Loans Are Currently In Repayment." Experian. https://www.experian.com/blogs/ask-experian/research/student-loan-debt-and-repayment/. October 15, 2019.

9 Federal Student Aid. https://studentaid.gov/manage-loans/forgiveness-cancellation.